PRIMARY FOUNDATION

History

AGES 7-9

Keith Andreetti
and Karin Doull

CONTENTS

Authors
Keith Andreetti and
Karin Doull

Editors
Clare Gallaher and
Sarah Snashall

Assistant Editor
Jean Coppendale

Series designer
Lynne Joesbury

Designer
Clare Brewer

Illustrations
Amanda Abbit/
illustrationweb

Cover photograph
Martyn Chillmaid

**Published by
Scholastic Ltd,**
Villiers House,
Clarendon Avenue,
Leamington Spa,
Warwickshire
CV32 5PR
**Visit our website at
www.scholastic.co.uk**
Text © 2000 Keith
Andreetti and Karin
Doull; © 2000
Scholastic Ltd
1 2 3 4 5 6 7 8 9 0
0 1 2 3 4 5 6 7 8 9

3
Introduction

7
Chapter 1 – Romans, Anglo-Saxons and Vikings in Britain
The Romans
The Anglo-Saxons
The Vikings

37
Chapter 2 – Britain and the wider world in Tudor times
Henry VIII
The Elizabethan Age

65
Chapter 3 – World history
Ancient Egypt
Benin – an African kingdom

92
Photocopiables

British Library Cataloguing-in-Publication Data
A catalogue record for this book is available from
the British Library.

ISBN 0-439-01809-9

Introduction

This book suggests how history can be divided into manageable teaching units for seven- to nine-year-olds. Each themed chapter provides two (or three, in the case of Chapter 1) units of work. These units are often complementary to each other and therefore you should choose one or other as appropriate to your needs. Most of the units can be used to form the basis of a substantial chunk of history work – perhaps over a half term – and by providing progressive lesson plans show how history can be sequenced. The grids at the beginning of each unit are intended to aid medium-term planning. They highlight (in bold) the enquiry questions covered by the lesson plans as well as additional enquiry questions which could be used to extend the unit further. The grids can also be used to help plan links that history has with other subjects across the curriculum, especially literacy and numeracy. (ICT links are given within the lesson plans themselves.) By providing a broad overview, the grids also help with planning the resources that you will need to collect in preparation for the unit.

The introductions to each unit provide some background information that you may find useful when working with the lesson plans, and further information is given in the lesson plans themselves.

Why is history important?

Before a subject can be taught well the teacher must understand what is most important and why it is important. History sometimes suffers from the fact that teachers do not always stop to consider its purpose. It is just 'there'. The National Curriculum Handbook for teachers starts the history section with four quotations that give some very good reasons for teaching history. They can be summarised as follows:

● History is about people; it allows us to examine the ways people behave, the ways in which they live and the things that happen to them and shows us that we belong to a rich tapestry of humanity.

● History is the science of story; it requires us to analyse and evaluate, to examine points of view and deduce motivation, to argue about morality and pronounce on character, all in the exciting virtual world of the past.

● History is about identity; it shows us why the world is as it is and presents our common heritage from which we can choose the elements on which to model ourselves and the world we want to create.

● History has endless content, and it can provide high-quality material for developing literacy, artistic and musical skills and can often link strongly with other subjects in the curriculum.

History for seven- to nine-year-olds

The teacher of seven- to nine-year-olds has two main priorities in teaching history. The first is to lay the foundations of historical skills and understanding, and monitor progression in them. (The Attainment Target gives guidance on how to do this.) The second is to begin to teach some solid information. The lesson plans given in this book have learning objectives which are designed to develop the required abilities in children, and the content of the activities is based on solid historical evidence.

Skills and understanding
1 Chronological understanding

Children at this age should already be familiar with timelines and they should have done a fair bit of sequencing in different contexts. The task now is to move towards the more formal historical framework. We begin to talk about Roman times and Saxon times and so on. You should use a few dates as markers along the way. It does not matter especially that the children can reel off a string of dates (though some children enjoy this) but they should be encouraged to count the

number of years between events and periods. This helps them as they start to relate one historical period to another.

Children need to understand the basic sequence of events within the period studied and also the sequence of periods. They should be encouraged to make comparisons between periods at every stage, particularly in relation to familiar things like clothes, houses and so on.

Increasingly they should be realising that things changed *within* the periods. Early Saxons were very different from the later Christian, literate English; Elizabethan England had moved on from Henry VIII's time in many ways.

2 Knowledge and understanding of events, people and changes in the past

For infants the emphasis was on giving a general flavour of life in different times. It is important in lower Key Stage 2 to discuss events in a much more coherent and linear way. We need to link events together to show how one thing leads to another. Rather than just accepting reasons from us, the children need to begin to suggest 'reasons why' for themselves on the basis of evidence. They need to understand, increasingly, that there are often a number of factors in play and that there are no simple answers.

3 Historical interpretation

Children need to understand that the people writing the stories and films like *Shakespeare in Love* or *Gladiator* (obviously, you would select sequences from the films that you consider suitable for your class) and creating the museum displays or reconstructions like the Globe theatre had to find out about the past from original sources. The lesson plans in this book introduce original sources alongside modern representations and the children should be encouraged to think about how accurate the modern representations are and what has been included or left out.

Each topic covered in this book presents different points of view – the Roman view as against Beric's British one, or the view of the Armada from Catholic Europe as opposed to Elizabeth's England. Learning that there are two sides to a question is probably the greatest gift history can give us and it will be a cruel waste if we neglect to use every opportunity to teach this life skill.

4 Historical enquiry

It is this element that points up the difference between history and fiction. History really happened and we find out about it by looking for evidence. It is important therefore to teach the concept of historical enquiry and lay a foundation of enquiry skills using different sorts of evidence.

Local history

The local environment is an essential source of historical evidence. Resources are rich, varied and available but often you need to find and prepare them yourself for the children's use. Increasingly children should be trying to use original material, but in the topics covered in this book translation is often required. It is important to develop your own knowledge of the local area and the possibilities that it holds for study. It is also important to find out about local history records and archives and how to access the information they contain. The local history library or County Record Office is the first and best source of material, and the local history librarian will be your guide to its treasures.

Finding out about the past from a range of sources

Sources are sometimes divided into primary sources and secondary sources. Primary ones are 'firsthand evidence', material actually from the time being studied – old photographs, for instance. Secondary sources are created later than the time they describe, like historical novels, history books or computer simulations. Primary sources like old photographs and artefacts have a patina of age and they help children understand that history is about things that really happened. Different sorts of sources need to be introduced and the children taught to use them.

● *Eyewitness accounts:* In the periods studied in this book we cannot talk directly to eyewitnesses

but there are plenty of documents containing such accounts and these are excellent for giving a particular point of view of the situation. Ibn Fadlan's viking funeral is a good example (pages 112–13).

- *Pictures:* These are excellent sources for the detail of costume, housing and so on. In many cases you will be using pictures from books that have been drawn from evidence but there are also some good original picture sources suggested in this book. Tudor portraits are a wonderful resource of this type.
- *Artefacts:* An artefact is anything made by human hands. Old things allow us to touch the past and help us to imagine those past people who held the object before us. In the periods studied in this book you will usually have to go to a museum to access artefacts of the correct period. Roman objects, in particular pottery, are comparatively common, though, and you might be able to get a loan collection from a museum to handle in school.
- *Museums, buildings and archaeological sites:* The secret of a successful history visit is to know exactly what your learning intentions are and to go to the right place at the right time to do the right things. Generally children will respond much better and achieve more if they understand that they are going on a trip to find answers from evidence. This means that often the best time for the trip is a little way into the topic, when the children are already involved and have formulated questions they want answered.

The activities they engage in at the museum, building or site should involve really looking at and thinking about the evidence. To do this the children must be able to see clearly and spend at least ten or fifteen minutes concentrating on each exhibit or display or area. This can be achieved by children being split into groups of six or seven, each with adult supervision.

Think about the questions that you will use to focus the children's investigation. It is important to encourage them to justify their answers, for example *Why do you think that? How do you know that?* rather than just asking for pieces of information. If it is allowed, use a camera (digital ones allow you more flexibility) to record different aspects of a visit. Recording answers and impressions on a cassette for later processing maximises valuable time.

5 Organisation and communication

Increasingly you should be looking for coherent written work that deals with historical issues and questions. The QCA booklet 'Expectations in History' is very helpful in giving an idea of the average expected from each year group. The children should be selecting and combining information from sources and using historical vocabulary. Obviously there is plenty of scope for combining this work with practice of general writing skills from the National Literacy Strategy.

Breadth of study

During Key Stage 2, children have to practise their knowledge, skills and understanding whilst studying six units. There is no statutory order for these, but most schools are following the more or less chronological pattern used by the QCA schemes. The chapters in this book therefore cover the units most often addressed in Years 3 and 4 and give sample lesson plans together with ideas for more. The current guidelines are clear that teachers should not try to be too comprehensive in their coverage of periods. It is better to cover smaller areas in some depth than to rush through vast chunks of history. This book gives choices of units using alternative content that provide roughly similar work in skills and understanding. Your choices may depend on supplementary material available in the local area, the children's interests or your own enthusiasms and knowledge.

Cross-curricular links

History has natural links with many other areas of the curriculum and the planning grids in this book provide examples of where specific links can be made. However, it is worth detailing some of the areas of the curriculum where ties with history are particularly strong and/or important.

History and literacy

While the focus of a Literacy Hour should be literacy, the use of historical texts can enhance it. Such texts may have interesting uses of vocabulary, tenses or reported speech. Texts of all types can be found: fiction, non-fiction, letters, poems and so on. If a suitable text is used in a morning's Literacy Hour, later, in history time, the children have as a starting point a well-understood story. It is for this reason that some texts have been provided in this book.

History and ICT

History and ICT also have much to offer one another but individual activities may not have equal 'pay off' in each subject. Sometimes those applications that are most useful in promoting good history do not develop the child's ICT skills very much and vice versa. It is important therefore to be clear in your learning intentions as to whether the activity is primarily history or ICT.

Word processing and desktop publishing: These applications are obviously invaluable to history. This will mainly be in connection with organising and communicating the children's knowledge of history, for example making history books, labels for wall displays, historical newspapers as well as straightforward pieces of writing.

Simulations: There are a number of history simulations designed for Key Stage 2 children. Some are very close in style to leisure games and the history content is largely window-dressing; others use virtual locations in an imaginative way to explore historical situations. The best advice is to try them yourself and evaluate them against historical knowledge, skills and understanding.

Databases and datafiles: Database work with programs like *Information Workshop* is desirable. Children could make data cards, including information gathered about historical figures or places. More modern software will allow pictures to be included. There are also prepared datafiles on CD-ROMs and encyclopaedias.

Timelines: There are one or two packages available that operate in the same way as a timeline on a wall, except that it scrolls across the screen. Children can enter material, and on the more modern ones they can scan in photographs and so on. Information gained in topics can be entered and accumulated on the class timeline program. It should not replace the wall-mounted timeline, however, which has the advantage of being visible at all times.

Multimedia: Packages like *Hyperstudio* probably offer the most exciting way forward because they allow the teacher and sometimes the child to create their own ICT resources. The basic model is of a stack of blank 'cards' on which text or pictures can be placed.

The Internet: There is a growing body of information now on the Internet, including a large number of original historical documents. Many lesson plans in this book give relevant websites. You should always check websites yourself before allowing the children to access them as some are more suitable and easier to use than others.

History and citizenship/PSHE

Part of citizenship/PSHE involves children in 'learning to understand and respect our common humanity, diversity and differences'. History allows us to develop this understanding in a number of ways. It allows us to view the rich diversity of human experience over different periods of time. By investigating events in the past, children can consider social and moral dilemmas and question people's emotions and motivations and also consider the consequences of choices made. In investigating historical characters children can discuss the rights and wrongs of their actions.

It is important to give children a wide selection of different people to investigate – women as well as men, black as well as white. This will allow children to appreciate both the diversity and commonality of human experience and to try to see the relevance in relation to their own lives.

Romans, Anglo-Saxons and Vikings in Britain

Since the original 'Invaders and Settlers' unit in the first set of National Curriculum orders there has been some confusion about the amount of ground to be covered in this unit. Many schools attempted to give an even coverage of the whole period and thus ended up with insufficient time to achieve any depth of study. In fact, the requirement has always been that *one* of the three peoples should be studied in detail. It is equally true, however, that you are required to give an 'overview' of the whole period.

The three units given in this chapter aim to meet the requirements of the orders fully. Each unit suggests several 'in-depth' lesson plans for the people chosen as the main focus; some lesson plans appear on more than one grid and these provide links between the people mentioned. A 'timeline' is provided at the beginning of each unit in this chapter, so that an informed overview can be achieved.

The whole period spans one thousand years, and any treatment of it in 15 or so lessons must be very selective. The reasons for and circumstances of the invasions are key areas of study. We are also required to look at 'How British society was affected'. This must mean learning about the characteristic features of everyday life in the period, and also its long-term legacy in terms of place-names, physical remains and cultural remnants such as the names we use for the days of the week.

Archaeology is very important in providing evidence of the period, and lessons are included for each option which uses such evidence. There is a small but important body of documentary evidence also and extracts have been rather freely translated and adapted for children of Years 3 and 4.

Roman Britain covers the first 400 years of the period and it links to the Anglo-Saxons as the demise of the one civilisation was connected with the rise of the other. The Anglo-Saxon period tends to fall into two distinct halves – pre- and post-Christian conversion – and a good part of the latter half is dominated by the Viking threat. Viking Britain is concurrent with Anglo-Saxon England and cannot really be treated in isolation from it.

The stories form an important part of these units because they put the evidence in a human context. They will help children to understand that real people with real feelings were involved. Many of them can be photocopied onto acetates and used for shared reading in the Literacy Hour. (The timings in the activities do not include the reading of the stories.)

Schools should ideally make their choice of which people to study in depth in the light of the availability of local evidence in museums, sites or in the landscape. This would mean that there is little scope for in-depth study of the Vikings if your school is in the south of England, as the Vikings did not occupy that area. The Romans are often the easiest choice simply because such a lot of material evidence survives. The Romans used bronze, glass and stone, all of which last well in the ground, whilst the Anglo-Saxon goods of leather and wood rotted away. Once the choice is made, you can study a map and get out into the area to look for the local evidence. Photo and picture packs are invaluable resources, especially with this age group. Apart from providing specific evidence to interpret, they give children a feel for the period and what it looked like. A wide variety of resource books is needed to allow children to research aspects of life and access different representations and interpretations of the past.

It must be said lastly that the units of study in this chapter necessarily involve discussion of violence and warfare. This, in most cases, is happily beyond the experience of the children in your class. It is, however, very much part of daily news in our time. History provides a context in which we can examine violent conflict from a safe distance. Children should be encouraged to look for opposing points of view and, hopefully, come to understand both that right is seldom all on one side and that actions can have serious consequences.

The Romans

The period of Roman Britain spanned 400 or so years. In terms of technology and standards of material comfort, the rich of that period lived in ways not equalled until Victorian times. Because of the permanent materials used in many buildings and the sheer number of 'things' made of substances like pottery and bronze, which can show little deterioration, we have lots of evidence of life in the period.

55BC   Julius Caesar invaded Britain, then went away again.

AD43   The Emperor Claudius finished what Caesar had started and colonised Britain.

AD49   The Foundation of Colchester/Camelodunum. When the Romans decided to stay and incorporate a province into the Empire, they founded coloniae, model towns where retired legionaries were encouraged to settle, thus creating an urban population loyal to the Empire to disseminate the Roman way of life.

AD60 or 61   Boudica led Iceni and Trinovantes tribes in revolt, burning Colchester, St Albans and London and giving the Romans a bad fright. But the governor of Roman Britain, Seutonius Paulinus, returned quickly from his massacres in Anglesey to defeat her.

AD117   Hadrian became Emperor. He built Hadrian's Wall, which symbolised the boundary of Roman civilisation. Hadrian came to power at the point when the Empire stopped being a constantly expanding colossus, and began to concentrate more and more on defending its vast territories against the massed 'barbarians' outside its borders. The wall is the ultimate symbol of this. The Emperor came to Britain personally to supervise its construction.

AD235–70   From this time on, the Roman Empire was constantly preoccupied with maintaining its borders against wave after wave of invaders, first Goths then Huns. Increasingly, the Western Empire was separated from the Eastern. The provinces of Britain became more and more of a separate entity. The Empire used large numbers of 'barbarian' troops, and graves along Hadrian's Wall show that Saxons were already coming to Britain, first as regular legionaries, then as feoderati or mercenaries allowed to settle here. Heavy defensive walls were added to many Roman cities in Britain, including Londinium, Noviomagus (Chichester) and Eburacum (York).

AD306   The Emperor Constantine the Great was proclaimed at York. Constantine restored the Empire for a while to some of its former greatness. He made himself sole Emperor, and built Roma Nova at Byzantium, which survived as Constantinople (now Istanbul). He is probably most famous for adopting (and adapting) Christianity as the state religion. There is evidence of Christian worship in Britain some time before this and other religions continued here afterwards. By the 4th century the focus of the Roman world had moved to Constantinople, and the Goths became more and more powerful in Italy. Imperial influence came and went in Britain but increasingly there is evidence of fortification of towns and villas against barbarian raids (Saxon, Pictish and Irish), and the withdrawal of regular troops from Britain. Local rulers started acting more and more like kings.

AD409   The last units of the XX Victoria Victrix legion probably left from Richborough, leaving Britain without all the administrative infrastructure that the Roman army provided as well as no effective defence against the gathering barbarians.

UNIT: The Romans

Enquiry questions	Learning objectives	Teaching activities	Learning outcomes	Literacy links	Cross-curricular links
Who lived in Britain before the Romans?	• Learn about some aspects of life in pre-Roman Britain.	Group reading of story about the coming of the Romans on pages 92–3. Teacher-led discussion about aspects of life and reasons for the Roman victory. Draw pictures illustrating story using source pictures.	Children: • draw accurate representations of some aspects of Celtic life	Read information passage and identify key points.	ICT: Use word processing to create captions for pictures. Design and technology: make a model of Beric's farmstead.
Why did the Romans invade Britain?	• Give some reasons for the Roman invasion and examine some ways in which it has been represented.	Teacher-led discussion about Roman Empire using a map. Group work using extracts from documentary sources and fact file sheets. Plenary discussion of reasons for the invasions.	• list factual information from the accounts • apply this information to the general question of why the Romans invaded • pass a reasoned opinion on the merits of the sources	Read information passages and identify main points. Make a simple record of information from text read. Report writing on conclusions.	ICT: create a database from document fact file.
What was it like to live in a Roman villa?	• Combine information from various sources; learn about some aspects of Roman life.	Combine information from villa plan, story and other sources to identify key features.	• put together information from various sources about villa life	Read information passages and identify main points. Make a simple record of information from text read.	Art: design mosaics. Design and technology: make plans of villa and rooms.
What was life like in Roman towns?	• Combine information from various sources; learn about some aspects of Roman life.	Prepare pictures, plans and written explanations of features of town.	• put together information from various sources about town life	Read information passages and identify main points.	ICT: multimedia presentation of Roman town.
The Roman army	• Combine information from various sources; learn about some aspects of Roman life.	Teacher input about the Roman army. Children make shields and practise Roman drill.	• give some information about the life of a Roman soldier	Read instructions for drill. Write portrait of Roman soldier character.	Design and technology: make Roman wax tablets.
Why was Hadrian's Wall built?	• Give some reasons for the building of Hadrian's Wall.	Use *Hadrian's Wall* by Iain Watson (English Heritage) and OS map to talk about the wall; writing as follow-up.	• understand how and why the wall was built.	Read information passages and identify main points.	Citizenship: think about the lives of people living at a different time.
Why did the Anglo-Saxons come to Britain?	*see* Anglo-Saxons grid on page 19.				
Where did the Anglo-Saxons settle?	*see* Anglo-Saxons grid on page 19.				
What do we know about early Anglo-Saxon life?	*see* Anglo-Saxons grid on page 19.				
How did the Anglo-Saxons become the English?	*see* Anglo-Saxons grid on page 19.				
Why was King Alfred called 'the Great?'	*see* Anglo-Saxons grid on page 19.				

1 hour Who lived in Britain before the Romans?

Learning objective
Learn about some aspects of life in pre-Roman Britain.

Lesson organisation
Whole-class introduction, then individual work.

Vocabulary
Celts
Romans
invasion
warrior

Background information

Britain was part of the Celtic world before the Romans came, which means mainly that its people spoke languages of the Celtic family. Welsh and Breton are the surviving descendants of the Brittonic language. The Celts were a successful people who had swept across Europe in the first millennium BC. They sacked the city of Rome in 390BC. But theirs was not a unified empire, rather it was a group of peoples sharing language and culture. They were not literate so they left no contemporary accounts of themselves. The earliest Celtic documents are from the early Christian era. Some of these clearly record very ancient stories and they give a flavour of Celtic thought. Archaeology shows that Celtic Britain was largely rural. Extended families probably occupied stockaded farm sites with characteristic round, thatched houses. Hillforts or other defensive sites surrounded by ditches and banks were probably used to collect people and animals together in dangerous times. Roman writers refer to the tribes of Britain and kings and other aristocracy.

The Celts employed the 'heroic' method of fighting. Later Irish epics give accounts that probably give a good idea of the way the British fought. Aristocrats in light wicker chariots would race around looking for a worthy opponent among the enemy. When they found one they would leap off and have a duel while their charioteer took the chariot back out of the way. Ordinary warriors relied on a terrifying charge, with warpaint and lots of battle cries. There is a fair amount of evidence that Celtic women sometimes took part in war. Boudica, the warrior queen who led the revolt of AD61, is an obvious example but both Caesar and Tacitus say that British women fought sometimes. The Irish epics also refer to women warriors – as exceptions rather than as the rule, however.

The Romans relied on disciplined ranks of well-armoured foot soldiers operating as one, and they regularly routed much larger armies of barbarians.

What you need and preparation

Collect together some pictures and resources relating to pre-Roman Britain. Butser Ancient Farm in Hampshire is a long-running piece of experimental archaeology where a Celtic farmstead has been reconstructed from archaeological evidence. School visits are welcomed and it is highly recommended for a visit. Their web address is www.skcldv.demon.co.uk/iafintro.htm. Their website is quite small (at the time of writing) but it has photographs of the reconstructions and other written information. In addition, find pictures of Roman soldiers from the 1st century. There are many good books on the Roman army. *Warriors of Rome* by Michael Simkins is an excellent book with useful pictures. You will also need: photocopiable pages 92–3; board or flip chart; Blu-Tack; paper; writing and drawing materials.

What to do

15 mins Introduction

Read the story on photocopiable pages 92–3 to the children. Tell them that it recounts the thoughts of a fictional character called Beric on what it might have been like at the time the Romans invaded Britain and is not a genuine firsthand account. Focus first on the way information is given about the British way of life – the construction of the houses, the farmstead and the social structure. Encourage the children to notice particular words and phrases such as *cone of the thatched roof, wood fire, bannocks* (round, flat, unsweetened cakes), *torc* (a necklace or armband), *woad, roundhouse, farmstead, wooden stockade.* Secondly focus on the different ways of fighting depicted and the reasons for the Roman victory. Point out words and phrases such as *chariots, bronze shields, war patterns, wall of square shields, hail of spears* and so on. Now refer to the pictures you have collected to clarify what the houses and people probably looked like.

30 mins **Development**
Ask the children to draw a picture illustrating one scene from the story and provide them with suitable source pictures to give accurate detail. Encourage them to draw different scenes including:

● Beric waking up in the roundhouse
● the scene outside the roundhouse
● the chief in his war chariot
● the Dobunni war band riding along a track through the woods
● the battle
● Beric riding home.
Explain that they can add captions to their finished pictures, perhaps quoting from the story.

15 mins **Plenary**
Select some of the children's pictures and sequence them on the board, using Blu-Tack. Pick out accurate detail for comment.

Differentiation
This activity can be differentiated by outcome – some children will need very clear directions and source pictures which can be directly copied, whilst others will be able to make more use of their imagination.

Assessing learning outcomes
Do the pictures show accurate representations of some aspects of Celtic life?

ICT opportunities
Ask the children to word-process their captions.

Follow-up activities
● Convert the children's sequenced story pictures into a permanent display.
● Create life-size collage pictures of Celtic and Roman warriors (make a template for the outline shape by drawing around a child whom you have asked to lie down on the back of a sheet of wallpaper, cut roughly to the correct size).

---

1 hour Why did the Romans invade Britain?

Background information
In the 1st century AD the Roman Empire was already huge. It included most of the Mediterranean world and extended north to the Rhine. Control of this vast area, in a time long before radio, telegraph or motorised transport, relied on a road network and the disciplined legions that guarded it and marched along it. The protection and stability that Roman military might afforded meant that the standard of living of the well-off was unprecedented. Piped water and drains, public-heated baths, elegant stone architecture, shops containing goods from around the Empire and comparatively fast, efficient road transport were all available not just in Rome but in provincial towns. Such a standard of living was not reached again in Europe until the 19th century. We know a lot about the Roman world both from its extensive literature and the wealth of archaeological evidence.

There were at least three reasons why the Romans extended their Empire:
● The prosperity of the Roman world acted like a magnet to neighbouring barbarians; often the easiest way to stop raiding was to conquer and civilise the raiders. Caesar mentioned that the Britons were always helping the Gauls to attack Roman towns.
● All empires need raw materials and food sources for their cities. According to the Roman geographer Strabo, Britain was a source of cattle, corn, metals and slaves (among other things). The Roman Empire needed vast numbers of slaves to maintain its lifestyles, and wars were a good way to get them.
● Roman politicians achieved popularity in Rome by displays of military prowess. Claudius wanted a 'triumph', a military parade following a new conquest, and Britain was a convenient target.

In 55BC and again in 54BC Julius Caesar sailed across the Channel and fought one or two engagements with British tribes. He seems mainly to have been concerned with frightening them

Learning objectives
● Give some reasons for a historical event.
● Examine some ways in which the past is represented.

Lesson organisation
Whole class, then groups of about four mixed-ability groups, each with at least one good reader, are preferable.

Vocabulary
invasion
empire
exports
Gaul

with a show of force and with aiding pro-Roman locals into power. He sailed away with promises of tributes to be paid and did not return.

In the next 89 years there was talk of a proper invasion; the Emperor Caligula even assembled a fleet ready to sail. Caligula was murdered by his bodyguard and his stuttering Uncle Claudius was selected as a quick replacement (read *I, Claudius* by Robert Graves, Penguin). Claudius needed to make a quick impression on the public and the army and in AD43 he ordered the general Aulus Plautius to invade.

What you need and preparation

Find some visual resources for the Romans, such as PCET posters or other large pictures. There is a map of the Roman Empire around the time of the invasion at www.jmiller.demon.co.uk/empire.html. Prepare a sheet which provides the framework for a fact file (see 'Development' below) and make photocopies of it. You will also need: copies of photocopiable pages 94–5, cut into separate sections; writing materials.

What to do

Introduction
15 mins With the whole class, brainstorm what they already know about the Romans, and use some visual resources to provide cues. Emphasise the main points from the background information above and use a map of Europe to show the extent of the Roman Empire. Give a brief account of the invasion of Britain, and talk about the three main reasons given.

Development
30 mins Give out one account of the Roman invasion of Britain (copied and cut out from photocopiable pages 94–5) to each group, making sure that groups are given different accounts. Explain that the children should read their account and fill out a fact file sheet for it:

> Name of source
> Who wrote it?
> When was it written?
> Is it a contemporary source? (Was the writer alive at the time of the events he or she is describing?)
> List of the main facts in the document

Plenary
15 mins Let the groups report back on the information in their accounts and gather reasons for the Roman invasions. Summarise these on the board (see 'Background information'). Talk about the accuracy of the information in the accounts. (Suetonius was writing later than the events but he worked for the Emperor and understood how emperors thought. Caesar was actually there but he had reason to be biased. Strabo had no axe to grind but he was in Greece and was relying on other people's accounts.)

Differentiation

The accounts can be used in different ways. You may want to give two or all three accounts to an able group. Strabo's account is shorter and simpler and could be used for a less literate group.

Assessing learning outcomes

Can the children list factual information from the accounts? Can they apply this factual information to the general question of why the Romans invaded? Can they pass a reasoned opinion on the merits of the sources?

1 hour What was it like to live in a Roman villa?

Background information

The Romans occupied Britain for nearly 400 years so it is difficult to generalise about the whole period. Excavations of towns in Roman Britain show that they were small compared to other parts of the Empire, and Britain was undoubtedly a largely rural province. The villa was the big house at the centre of a colonial farm. Villa owners might be Celtic aristocracy who had adopted Roman ways as well as retired army officers or officials. Early villas were often timber-framed and thatched but masonry walls and tiles were increasingly used. Only the very rich could afford mosaic floors and wall paintings in the early days, but they became more commonplace as time went on. The other great status symbols were heated bathhouses and hypocausts. The latter was a form of underfloor heating. The fire was made in a grate in the outside wall of the house and the hot air was drawn under the mosaic floor and up flues built into the walls.

Slaves were an important part of life and a number of slaves would be needed to run even a small villa.

A visit to a Roman villa is highly recommended. Many have been excavated and most parts of the country are within reach of a villa which is open to the public (in the very north of England and the south of Scotland military sites are more common). There is a list of villas on www.athenapub.com/britmus2.htm; or use the Ordnance Survey map of Roman Britain. Fishbourne is probably the most famous but remember that it is not really a villa at all. It is usually described as a palace and it is certainly not typical. Mosaics seem to be one of those things that fascinate children and you should make use of their interest, but mosaics may tell us less about villa life than the hypocaust or baths.

What you need and preparation

Gather together some source pictures and information; pictures of mosaics are easy to find and Guy de la Bedoyere's *The Buildings of Roman Britain* (Batsford) has pictures and useful information. Shire Publications have published some suitable little books, including *Roman Villas* by David Johnson. The Museum of London has a good reconstruction of a Roman kitchen and a picture of it is obtainable in their photo pack. You will also need: photocopiable pages 96–7; an enlarged copy of photocopiable page 98, plus individual A4 copies; board or flip chart; writing and drawing materials.

What to do

15 mins Introduction

Read the story on photocopiable pages 96–7 to the children and discuss the content. Help them to make a link with the story they heard in 'Who lived in Britain before the Romans' (see photocopiable pages 92–3) by reading the first couple of paragraphs from it to remind them of the house where Beric lived before the Romans came. Talk about how Beric has now become a slave and how he feels about it. Tell them that most private teachers were also slaves; they were often educated Greeks whose families had fallen on hard times.

Learning objectives
• Combine information from various sources.
• Learn about some aspects of Roman life in Britain.

Lesson organisation
Class introduction followed by individual work; individual or group research.

Vocabulary
villa
hypocaust
slave
courtyard
mosaic
Londinium

30 mins **Development**
Move on to look at the geography of the villa and use other pictures to illustrate the plan on the enlarged copy of photocopiable page 98. Talk about the fact that some rooms were heated with a hypocaust and others were not, for example the winter dining room. Explain that the walls were often painted in bright colours. Talk about the mosaic floors. Ask why the children think the kitchen was in a separate house (this may have been to avoid fire risks or it may have been a way of keeping the slaves' working areas away from the family). Talk about the elaborate bathhouse which was like a sauna – this would be for family and guests only.

Now distribute copies of photocopiable page 98 and ask the children to answer the questions on the sheet, working individually.

Divide the children into groups and give out reference material. Explain that each group will research what different parts of the villa may have looked like, then draw a picture of the part of the villa that they have found out about. For example, some children could find out about the kitchen and what it looked like inside; some could draw the outside or the inside of the bathhouse; the Roman family at dinner with men reclining and women on chairs would make another subject.

Follow-up activities
● Show the children how to construct a model of a villa using a basic box shape and referring to the ground plan on photocopiable page 98.
● Ask the children to design mosaics for the floors.

15 mins **Plenary**
Invite the groups to show their pictures to the rest of the class and report back on what different parts of the villa were like. Display the enlarged copy of photocopiable page 98 in the centre of the flip chart and add key information around the villa plan.

Differentiation
The research can be differentiated by the source material given, from basic copying from pictures to reading and interpreting written information.

Assessing learning outcomes
Can the children put together information from various sources about villa life? Do they know something about life in a Roman villa?

What was life like in Roman towns?

Learning objectives
● Combine information from various sources.
● Learn about some aspects of Roman life.

Background information
Although Roman Britain was largely rural there were a number of small and middle-sized towns. Modern names ending in *chester, caster* or *cester* are evidence that the Saxons found remains of a Roman *castra* or military camp on the site. Other major Roman centres were at London (Londinium), York (Eburacum), Exeter (Isca Dumniorum) and Wroxeter (Viriconium). Lincoln was *Lindum Colonia*; a *colonia* was a sort of model town settled with retired Roman soldiers and other immigrants, intended as an example of Roman culture and a loyal strongpoint in conquered territory. Most Roman towns continued to be occupied to a greater or lesser extent until the present day. They often have some visible Roman remains and their museums always have interesting material. Silchester (Calleva Atrebatum) in Berkshire is interesting in that it was abandoned at the end of the Roman period; the entire ground plan of the town survives as lumps and bumps in the ground, which make it a good venue for a field trip. The best source of material on Roman towns may well be the nearest one to you.

Key features of a Roman town were:
● the forum – this was the central square where markets were held
● the basilica – the law courts and council building, usually on one side of the forum

Lesson organisation
Class introduction; individual or group work on research.

- temples – to numerous deities
- baths – public baths were essential to civilised life and men spent a lot of time soaking, sweating and being massaged or depilated; they were also great centres for gossip and socialising
- arenas – for gladiatorial combat or beast fights; there were a number of small arenas in Britain
- theatres – remains of semicircular open-air theatres like Greek ones exist in some towns
- town walls – often these were not built until the end of Roman Britain when barbarians were attacking and the invincible reputation of the legions was waning; there are sections still standing in several towns.

What you need and preparation

If possible, gather information about your nearest Roman town. Contact the museum in the town to find out about what is available. Information might include a town plan. If you cannot find a local one there is a town plan of Caistor St Edmund, Norwich (Venta Icenorum) at www.sys.uea.ac.uk/Research/researchareas/JWMP/CaistorRomanTown/caistormap.gif. Try to find some artists' impressions of Roman towns. Again if you cannot find local examples there are nice ones of Silchester (Calleva) at www.hants.org.uk/leisure/history/calleva/index.html. You will also need: pictures of typical buildings (you will find plenty in Guy de la Bedoyere's *The Buildings of Roman Britain*, Batsford); a map of your region showing Roman sites (use the Ordnance Survey map of Roman Britain to prepare your own map with the level of detail that you feel is appropriate for your class, including towns, roads, known villas and military camps); board or flip chart; writing materials.

What to do

(15 mins) Introduction

Start by looking at a regional map of Roman Britain as a class and comparing it to the region today. Move on to look at the town plan and point out the main features.

(30 mins) Development

Ask the children to research what different parts of the town may have looked like, explaining that they will be drawing pictures, preparing plans and writing explanations of features of the Roman town. Provide them with the resources you have obtained, to use for reference; the basilica, the forum, the public baths and the arena would be good subjects for pictures (you can find models for all of these in Guy de la Bedoyere's *The Buildings of Roman Britain*).

(15 mins) Plenary

Invite groups or individuals to show their finished pictures to the rest of the class and to report back on what they have found out. Make brief written notes and Blu-Tack the information around the town plan on the board.

Differentiation

As in the previous activity, the research can be differentiated by the source material given and the tasks allocated.

Assessing learning outcomes

Can the children put together information from various sources about town life?

Vocabulary
forum
basilica
mures (walls)
castra
oppidum (town)

ICT opportunities
Use the activity as a basis for a *Hyperstudio* project. The town plan can be on the first 'card', with hidden buttons which take you to other cards containing scanned children's pictures and text. A recorded commentary can be added which might be written from the point of view of townspeople (see the next activity).

Follow-up activity
Ask the children to write about a tour of the Roman town by imagining themselves walking around the plan and describing what they can see, hear and smell. Produce a simple worksheet for less able children: *I am standing in the forum looking West. I can see…* Encourage imaginative writers to write a story which uses the town as its setting – perhaps they could be looking for someone, or imagine themselves as a runaway slave trying to avoid his master.

(1 hour) The Roman army

Background information

The army was the centre pin of the Roman Empire. It was the creation of a regular paid army under Marius (*c*155–86BC) that initiated the relentless expansion. Roman soldiers were trained and disciplined, well equipped and permanently available. Barbarian armies often had divided loyalties and they usually wanted to get home in time to harvest their crops. Once a barbarian army had charged, there was usually no way of controlling it. Roman soldiers obeyed set commands and trumpet signals. They owed allegiance to the Empire and perhaps even more to the Eagle Standard of their legion.

The Roman legionary carried a mattock or other tools as well as his weapons. In hostile territory the army could construct a fortified camp with earth walls, and ditch each night at the end of a long march. Roads followed the military. A swathe of forest was cut down each side to prevent ambush. Roads were raised up, both for easier defence and to prevent flooding. They were straight partly because it was easier to survey in straight lines but also to allow maximum visibility along the road. Signal stations manned by soldiers were strung out along the road so that a message could be sent with amazing speed. Soldiers could be moved along the roads to trouble spots easily and with great rapidity.

After 20 years in service, a soldier was entitled to a pension – this was theoretically in the form of a piece of land somewhere in a Roman colony. Thus loyal retired soldiers were planted out to spread Roman ways throughout the Empire.

What you need and preparation

Find some examples of Roman shields and swords; Roman re-enactment societies, in particular 'The Ermine Street Guard', are experts on the Roman Army and other aspects of Roman life. Make contact with local members through their website at www.esg.ndirect.co.uk. This site has images of people dressed in authentic uniforms. You may well be able to get a local member to visit the school in costume! Or perhaps the short-term loan of equipment could be arranged. There are useful pictures and information in *Warriors of Rome* by Michael Simkins (Osprey), and children's books with suitable pictures of Roman soldiers are always easy to find. You will also need: thick card (suitable for making shields – the sides of large cardboard boxes about 60cm x 45cm would be better than bought card); thick paint mixed with PVA glue (red and yellow are probably authentic colours); paintbrushes; a shield that you have made yourself, to use as a demonstration model (painted to resemble a picture of one that you have chosen); scissors; paper fasteners.

What to do

(15 mins) Introduction

Talk to the class about the Roman army, making the points mentioned in the background information above. If you have arranged for an Ermine Street legionary to visit

the children, it would be exciting if he walked in without warning at a pre-arranged signal! Alternatively, use pictures to talk through the basic equipment that a Roman legion required, such as the following:

- gladius – a short sword designed for stabbing from behind the shield wall
- scutum – a big squarish shield made to protect the whole body
- pilum – a javelin for throwing
- caligae – sandals with nails in the soles
- cuirass – body armour made of plates of iron
- helmet.

30 mins Development

Show the children the cardboard shield that you have made and demonstrate how to make their own using the cardboard sheets. Explain that they should draw the correct outline shape in pencil before cutting out their shield and painting it. Encourage them to refer to the source material you have prepared when they think about the design. When they have finished their shields, they can attach a cardboard strip to the back with paper fasteners to make a handle.

15 mins Plenary

Take the children to the school hall or playground, with their shields, and practise manoeuvres such as 'forming testudo'. *Testudo* is Latin for 'tortoise'. Soldiers learned to hold their shields in this formation in order to protect themselves when advancing through a hail of missiles. The information below is based on the Ermine Street Guard's drill manual. There is no absolute evidence about how the Roman army did it but the ESG have used carvings from Trajan's column and other research to make informed guesses.

Practise forming fours to the order *Quattor ordines facite* (*kwattor ordinays fasitay*). The children should be in rows of four facing forward:

```
+   +   +   +
+   +   +   +
+   +   +   +
+   +   +   +
+   +   +   +
```

At this stage their shields will be against their left side. At the order *Intente* they should stand to attention. At the order *Testudo facite* the front four hold their shields in front of them. The rear four break off, with two children running forward up each side to hold their shields to protect the sides; everyone else holds their shields above their heads. At the order *Testudo procedite* the children advance slowly. At the order *Testudo discedite* shields go back to their original position and the children get back into fours. (Other orders are: *dextrosum vertite* – right turn; *sinistrorsum vertite* – left turn; *consistite* – halt.)

Assessing learning outcomes

Can the children give some accurate names and other information about the life of a Roman soldier?

> **ICT opportunities**
> Add further information to the cards on your *Hyperstudio* stack leading from a military building on the town plan (see previous activity).

The Anglo-Saxons

The Anglo-Saxon period commences in the chaos and uncertainty of the end of Roman rule (cAD410), and we know very little about the details. What we do know is a mixture of later legendary accounts mixed with archaeological evidence. We know that the Anglo-Saxons began to settle in the east and in little more than a hundred years they occupied most of present day England (excluding Cornwall) along with some of southern Scotland. These early dates and events are very much open to question.

AD455   Hengest's rebellion. Hengest, a Saxon mercenary leader, rebelled against his employer, Vortigern (a British chief) and founded the Jutish kingdom of Kent.

AD477   Aelle the Saxon conquers Sussex. The Saxon cemetery at Worthing shows that the wives of these Saxons wore Celtic jewellery which suggests that there was intermarriage between Celts and the Saxon mercenaries.

AD495   A band of Saxon adventurers under their leader, Cerdic, land in Southampton, capture Winchester and found the kingdom of Wessex.

ADc520   The Battle of Badon Hill. It has been recorded that a great victory by the Britons over the Saxon invaders was won at *Mons Badonicus* and archaeology seems to confirm that the incursions were checked for 40 to 50 years. The great leader who achieved this may have been Arthur.

AD597   St Augustine is sent to England by Pope Gregory to convert the 'English'. With Christianity came literacy and we begin to have contemporary written accounts after this date. The word *English* is increasingly used to describe the descendants of the Angles, Saxons, Jutes and so on.

AD624   Death of Raedwald, king of East Anglia. The superb ship burial at Sutton Hoo is probably Raedwald's grave. It is full of artefacts that throw light on the life of one of the last great pagan kings.

AD731   Bede, a monk from Jarrow, finished his *History of the English Church and People*.

AD793   The year of the first raids by Vikings from Denmark.

AD871   Alfred the Great was crowned king of Wessex.

AD878   The Battle of Edington. The Danes were defeated, their leader christened and an arrangement made whereby they maintained influence over about half the country under the nominal overlordship of Alfred. The area was called the Danelaw, because it was under Danish law.

AD919   Viking kingdom of York founded.

AD1042   Edward the Confessor becomes king. Edward was a descendent of Alfred. He built Westminster Abbey and he is buried there.

AD1066   Edward dies. He had no heir; the Witan (council) elected Harold Godwineson as king. Immediately two other claimants emerged – Harald Hardrada, king of Norway and Duke William of Normandy. Harold Godwineson defeated the former at Stamford Bridge and lost to the latter at Hastings.

UNIT: The Anglo-Saxons

Enquiry questions	Learning objectives	Teaching activities	Learning outcomes	Literacy links	Cross-curricular links
Why did the Anglo-Saxons come to Britain?	• Give a few reasons for and results of the Anglo-Saxon invasions. • Answer questions about the past in ways that go beyond simple observations.	Group reading Witta's and Flavia's stories (photocopiable pages 99–100). Teacher-led discussion comparing points of view. Mini debate.	Children: • give some reasons why the characters acted as they did • give a reasoned opinion about the rights and wrongs of the situation	Use writing frame to note reasons and opinions.	Citzenship: think about the lives of people living at different times and people with different values and customs.
Where did the Anglo-Saxons settle?	• Use evidence from place-names to learn about Saxon settlement in the local area.	Teacher-led discussion about how English place-names originated. Pair or group work finding Saxon place-names on a local area map.	• find the Saxon derivations of local place-names • understand that such people lived in their local area	Label local maps with translations of Saxon names. Write two different first-person accounts of the same story.	Art: create a wall display of the local area. Geography: explain how settlements change using appropriate vocabulary and a variety of maps.
What do we know about early Saxon life?	• Use evidence from various sources to learn about Saxon everyday life.	Teacher input about Anglo-Saxon life and the process of archaeology. Group work: • examine pictures of artefacts from village sites. Discuss objects and reach conclusions. • examine pictures of Sutton Hoo finds. Discuss objects and reach conclusions. • use information books and pictures to gather details of Anglo-Saxon dress and objects. • use site plans in West Stowe leaflet to research Anglo-Saxon buildings.	• understand how archaeology provides evidence of early Anglo-Saxon life • use archaeological evidence to reach conclusions about it by simple observation and in ways that go beyond simple observation	Locate information using contents pages and index, headings and so on. Read information passages and identify main points.	Maths: visit West Stowe website, create nets of Anglo-Saxon buildings to make model village.
How did the Anglo-Saxons become the English?	• Make links and comparisons between the Anglo-Saxon period and the present.	Teacher input about the kingdoms of the Dark Ages and the peoples that became the English, Scottish and Welsh nations. Children identify characteristics of early English society and express opinions on it.	• pass a reasoned opinion about early English life	Present opinions with reasons in writing.	
How did the Anglo-Saxons become Christian?	• Use documentary evidence to find out about the conversion of the English to Christianity.	Use Bede's account of the coming of St Augustine and his conversion of Ethelbert, king of Kent. Children sequence and retell the story.	• sequence the story of St Augustine	Plot episodes in a known story. Write a play about St Augustine.	
Why is King Alfred called 'the Great'?	• Use documentary sources to identify different ways in which the past is represented. • Learn about a significant historical character.	Teacher tells story of King Alfred. Whole-class analysis of one account. Groups examine different accounts using text fact file. Plenary comparison and compilation of accounts.	• use sources to gather factual information about Alfred • give reasoned opinions about the merits of different accounts.	Identify main points from a passage. Make a simple record of information by completing fact file.	Art: illustrated display of Alfred's life.

50 Why did the Anglo-Saxons come to Britain?

Background information

In the 4th and 5th centuries the Roman Empire suffered increasingly from invasions by 'barbarians' (people they considered uncivilised). The real centre of the Empire had moved from Rome to Constantinople (now Istanbul), and Italy itself was raided and later conquered by Goths. Britannia, far off in the west, became increasingly independent of the Empire. More and more regular Roman soldiers were ordered away from Britain and mercenary 'federates' were hired to replace them. These mercenaries often belonged to Germanic tribes like the Saxons, Angles and Jutes. The mercenaries were allowed to bring their families and settle in areas of Britain. The Saxon mercenaries were given land along the coasts of southern and eastern Britain so that they could defend the coast against other Saxon raiders. The Romans built forts around the south-east coast to repel Saxon invaders.

At that time, these 'Anglo-Saxons' came from very poor land in Denmark, Holland and North Germany. It was a period of bad winters and high sea levels and some groups had to live on man-made hills called *terpen* because the land flooded so often. To these people Britain was a very attractive place to settle.

A lot of information about Britain is uncertain at this time, hence the period is often referred to as the 'Dark Ages'. However, we do know that some of the Roman towns like London and York and Caerleon were still quite prosperous and new walls and buildings continued to be erected. We have the names of a number of kings and rulers during this time and some of these have Roman names, but more have Celtic names. These rulers seem to have fought among themselves a lot and they rarely united to fight off the Saxon advance as they started to take more and more land. In this chaotic situation, not only Saxons but also Irish and Picts from Scotland raided Britain, stealing, taking people into slavery and destroying farms and villages. Saint Patrick was a Romano-British boy taken to Ireland as a slave in one of these raids.

One leader who might have united the British for a while was Arthur, but historians are very divided as to whether he really existed. Certainly we have nothing detailed written about him until nearly 300 years later.

The story of Vortigern and Hengest comes from the writing of the Welsh monk Gildas that was written about 50 years after the events described.

What you need and preparation

You will need: photocopiable pages 99, 100–1 and 102; writing materials.

What to do

20 Introduction

Read the stories on photocopiable pages 99 and 100–1 to the children, then follow the reading with a general discussion in which you establish that the accounts represent two points of view of the same event. Encourage the children to give reasons why Witta acted as he did and help them to explore how Flavia must have felt about the attacks on her home and the end of her comfortable life.

20 Development

Ask the children to complete the writing frame on photocopiable page 102, working either individually or in groups. They should use the accounts on photocopiable pages 99–101 to find out why Witta came to Britain and to think about whose fault it was that Flavia had to leave her home. For example:

I think it was Vortigern's fault because he was giving Saxons land and they were taking over more and more land. The Romans thought that the Saxons were barbarians and they did not trust them. Flavia's family wanted the Roman soldiers to defend them.

Witta came to Britain because where he lived, the land flooded and the crops did not grow, and the people starved. In England it was dry, the crops grew and the people looked fat and well-fed. Also, he wanted to be a warrior and the messenger said that Hengest, who worked for a king in England called Vortigern, needed some warriors to fight in a war band.

I think that it was the Saxons' fault because they were supposed to be protecting the Romans because Vortigern told them to. But they were getting drunk and raiding the villas because they wanted to get things to sell to buy ornaments and weapons.

 Plenary
Divide the class in half and organise a mini debate in which Witta's and Flavia's respective positions could be argued. One group should argue from Witta's viewpoint and the other from Flavia's. The children should be able to pick out the parts of the stories that support each point of view and express sympathy for the characters. Conclude that there are no simple rights and wrongs in historical questions.

Differentiation
Less able children can give oral answers to photocopiable page 102 instead of written ones, whereas more able children can use the writing frame and/or notes they have taken during the debate to write a full written account.

Assessing learning outcomes
Can the children give some of the reasons why the characters acted and thought as they did? Can they give a reasoned opinion about why the Anglo-Saxons came and whether it was right to do so?

ICT opportunities
Use a multimedia program such as *Hyperstudio* to make an interactive version of this activity. Include a voice recording of Witta's and Flavia's accounts and program it to store the responses of different groups or individuals, either written or voice recorded.

 # Where did the Anglo-Saxons settle?

Background information
Most English place-names are of Anglo-Saxon origin, although the majority of Welsh and Cornish place-names are Celtic and some areas like Lincolnshire, Yorkshire and Cumbria have a good number of Viking place-names. Scotland has quite a few Anglo-Saxon names in the south but increasingly they become Gaelic or Viking as you move north. Northern Ireland has largely Gaelic place-names.

Most place-names are one of two types – either they describe a geographical feature like a hill, wood or a ford on a river, or they give the name of the supposed founder of the settlement along with a suffix meaning 'farm' or 'village', or in some cases 'fortified place'. There has been some controversy about names ending in *ing*. Often this derives from *ingas* which means 'the people of', as in *Worthing* (the settlement of Weorth's people). Traditionally, these were thought to indicate an early settlement by an invading war band of Saxons. Many of these names are to be found along the Thames Valley and the Sussex coast but fewer in Kent. Some historians thought this

Learning objective
Use evidence from place-names to learn about Saxon settlement in the local area.

Lesson organisation
Whole-class introduction, followed by group or individual work.

Vocabulary
river
ford
hill
wood
moor
(Also see
photocopiable page
103–4 for suffixes
and prefixes.)

showed how the Saxons avoided Jutish Kent and spread out from water routes to found Sussex, Essex, Middlesex and Wessex. More recent research is cautious about this, and some *ing* names do not seem to derive from the word *ingas* at all. It is probably enough for children to realise that some place-names do survive from Saxon times, that we can guess at the names of some of those first invaders and that we can see how the geography of the area influenced settlement.

Further information can be found in AD Mills's *Oxford Dictionary of English Place-names* (OUP). The Victoria County Histories can usually be found in your local reference library and they may also be helpful.

What you need and preparation
Find a map of your local area; this must be of a suitable scale to give ten or so place-names to choose from and it should show the relevant geographical features (such as a 1/2500 Ordnance Survey map). You will also need: a map of the area south of Chichester in West Sussex (a road atlas will be adequate); photocopiable pages 103–4.

15 mins **Introduction**
Remind the children of the story about Witta (see photocopiable pages 99–101). Look at the map of the Chichester area and help them to recognise where the characters may have settled. Point out that the story is fictional but the place-names on the map prove that there were real people with those names who settled in the area.

Talk about how English place-names were formed, and introduce the prefixes and suffixes on photocopiable pages 103–4. Explain some of the derivations of the names on the map, for example *castra* is a Latin word meaning 'a Roman fort' and it survives in place-names ending in *caster, cester* and *chester*.

20 mins **Development**
Give pairs or groups of children access to the local map and ask them to find Saxon suffixes and to try to work out what the names might mean. Ask them to make a list of their translations of local place-names. (You may wish to use different adjoining maps to cover a greater area as a class and collect the results as a plenary activity.)

Follow-up activity
Carry out further research of place-names (see 'Background information') to check the children's ideas that they offered in the plenary.

10 mins **Plenary**
Encourage the children to guess why the settlements are placed in their geographical locations – look for their relationship to rivers, hills, Roman roads and so on. Make a list of possible names of early settlers in your locality.

Differentiation
The difficulty of the activity depends largely on the map used in the development session and the number of places included. A simplified map showing fewer places and only the key physical features could easily be prepared for less able children.

ICT opportunities
Prepare a database of local place-names and their derivations, as a class activity.

Assessing learning outcomes
Can the children find the Saxon derivations of local place-names and do they understand how they give evidence that Saxon people really lived in their local area?

(1 hour) What do we know about early Anglo-Saxon life?

Background information

Most of what we know about early Anglo-Saxon life in this country is based on archaeology. The Anglo-Saxons were almost entirely illiterate until the coming of Christianity so we have no material written by them at the time (except a few runic inscriptions). *Beowulf* is an epic poem that gives a flavour of pagan Anglo-Saxon culture, but it was not written down until later (cAD1000) and it is not set in England.

A number of Anglo-Saxon villages have been excavated and also a couple of early towns. At West Stow in Suffolk, village houses have been reconstructed on the site of archaeological excavations. The early Anglo-Saxons were not town dwellers and most settlements appear to have been small, probably being the holding of one prominent man and his extended family, followers and thralls (slaves).

Anglo-Saxon artefacts are not nearly as common in museums as those from Roman times. This is partly because they made a lot of things from organic materials like leather and wood that rot away quickly, and partly because they probably had fewer material possessions. The British Museum has the best collection of objects. Pots, conical glasses, small knives, bone combs and needles, beads and cross-shaped brooches are the more common finds, along with the pommels of swords and shield bosses.

Also to be found in the British Museum are the unique finds from the Sutton Hoo ship burial. This was probably the grave of a king (probably Raedwald, king of East Anglia), buried in a longship with his horse and prized possessions. It is quite late – he died about AD624 – and it contains rich objects that certainly do not represent the sorts of things that ordinary people used at the time. However, the finds do show the beauty and craftsmanship of which Anglo-Saxon society was capable. It is not difficult to obtain photographs of the Sutton Hoo finds – the famous helmet (with moustache) and belt buckle are particularly popular illustrations.

What you need and preparation

Gather together a collection of books which have illustrations of Anglo-Saxon life and photographs of artefacts that have been found on village sites such as bone combs, pins, spindle-whorls (doughnut-shaped clay weights on the end of spindles for spinning wool), brooches and pots. You will also need: photographs of the Sutton Hoo finds, for example in *The Sutton Hoo Ship Burial* by Angela Care Evans (British Museum Press); an Anglo-Saxon house plan (the West Stow Village Trust produce a small leaflet about the reconstructions that shows the evidence on which they were based); pictures of Anglo-Saxon artefacts found locally or elsewhere (your local museum may be able to help you with this); photocopiable page 105 (enlarged); paper; writing and drawing materials.

What to do

(15 mins) Introduction

Talk to the children about how we know about Anglo-Saxon life and the process of archaeology. Explain that there is hardly anything left today that was written at the time and discuss why they think this might be. Ask the children if they can think of any other ways we could find out about life at this time. Tell them that the houses Witta and his friends would have built (see photocopiable page 99) have all disappeared now and we do not have any photographs or pictures of them. But we do know where some of them were. The archaeologists begin with aerial photographs which show there could have been a settlement in the area. This gives clues about where to dig to find evidence of what the houses were like. Explain how the topsoil is

Learning objective
Use evidence from various sources to learn about Saxon everyday life.

Lesson organisation
Whole-class introduction followed by group or individual work.

Vocabulary
archaeology
site
post holes
artefacts
hall
shield boss
pommel
ard
thrall

removed to get down to the archaeological layers beneath. If the archaeologist is lucky, he or she may find objects, but often there are just dark marks on the ground to show where wooden posts were sunk, or burned earth where a fire was made. Show the children the plan of the Anglo-Saxon house on the enlarged copy of photocopiable page 105 and explain it. Ask key questions such as:

● What do you think the wooden posts were for? (The walls.)
● Why are there remains of a fire in the middle of the floor? (To heat the house and cook.)
● Why do you think there is an inner wall? (To form a bedroom for the head man and his wife?)
● How big was the house? (Use the scale to compare it to the classroom.)

Explain that the early Anglo-Saxons had to build with materials that they could find in the area, such as wood and straw. They did not have window glass. You may wish to bring in some straw (animal bedding from a pet shop) as children may not have seen and handled it. It is important to show that archaeologists make educated guesses from clues and we cannot be sure exactly what the house looked like.

(30 mins) Development

Tell the children that they are going to look at some illustrations of Anglo-Saxon life to gather information and produce drawings for a display. Divide them into three or four groups and give each group a different set of source material to investigate such as pictures of Sutton Hoo finds; photographs of artefacts – these might include tools such as axes and ards (ploughs) or spindles and looms, weapons and jewellery; information books containing details of Anglo-Saxon dress; plans of different buildings in an Anglo-Saxon village. Ask the children to draw carefully a picture of one aspect of Anglo-Saxon life, and explain that they will be sharing information about what they have drawn. Encourage them to write some brief notes about the object, if they can.

(15 mins) Plenary

Invite the groups to show their pictures to the rest of the class. Ask the children questions such as:

● What sort of people do you think would have used these things (male/female/rich/poor)?
● What do these things tell us about Anglo-Saxon life?
● What further information would you need to build a more accurate picture?
● How useful are they as a source?

Differentiation
By outcome – there will be variations in the expectations for written notes and plenary presentation.

Assessing learning outcomes
Can the children understand that we have to work out what Anglo-Saxon life was like by putting together archaeological clues? Have they gained some factual information about life in an Anglo-Saxon village?

ICT opportunities
● Visit the West Stow website at www.oldcity.demon.co.uk/stowfriends/aboutstow.html.

Follow-up activity
Include the children's drawings in a display about Anglo-Saxon life. Create life-size figures dressed in appropriate costume and adorned with suitable artefacts.

(1 hour) How did the Anglo-Saxons become the English?

Learning objective
Combine evidence from two sources to find out about early English society.

Background information
Anglo-Saxon settlement in eastern England started in the 5th century. During the next 100 years, most of present day England and some of southern Scotland was occupied as the Romano-British (called *Welsh,* meaning 'foreigners', by the Saxons) were pushed west. Prominent leaders set up kingdoms, first Kent, then Sussex, East Anglia, Wessex, Northumbria, Mercia and so on. The great English historian Bede in his *History of the English Church and People*, written in AD731, tells

us that different tribes formed the kingdoms. Sussex and Wessex (kingdoms of the South Saxons and West Saxons) were settled by Saxons from north Germany; Kent and the Isle of Wight by Jutes from north Denmark; and East Anglia, Mercia and Northumbria by Angles from south Denmark. Even though they were originally from different places, the settlers all spoke a similar language and had a shared culture. The Welsh hung on to modern Wales and Cornwall, Cumbria and Strathclyde. Gaelic-speaking Scots came from Ireland (confusingly enough) and settled in the Hebrides and the Western Highlands.

The map on photocopiable page 106 shows Celtic and Anglo-Saxon kingdoms that existed during this period. Borders moved and large kingdoms took over smaller ones so it is difficult to be specific about exactly when the map looked like this. It should be mentioned that these kingdoms quite often fought one another, and Celts and Saxons were often allies against other neighbours. The Welsh were driven out of Strathclyde and Rheged by the Saxons and Scots.

Saxon religion was similar to that of the Vikings and we preserve the names of Saxon gods in four days of the week: Tuesday – named after *Tiu*, god of war, son of Woden and younger brother of Thor; Wednesday – named after *Woden*, chief of the gods, god of wisdom and the dead; Thursday – named after *Thor*, son of Woden and god of thunder; Friday – *Frigg's day*, who was Woden's wife and goddess of the dead.

Though the Saxons initially established small agricultural settlements, it was not long before towns grew up again. Each king had one or more royal *burhs* (see the table of place-names on photocopiable page 103) where craftsmen and traders would gather to serve the aristocracy. Burhs were fortified centres that protected different areas from attack.

The consolidation of the kingdoms and the spread of literacy and Christianity increasingly created a sense of English identity. Though some earlier kings called themselves king of England, Alfred was the first with a real claim to do so.

Lesson organisation
Whole-class introduction followed by individual or group work.

Vocabulary
Picts
Scots
Strathclyde
Northumbria
Mercia
East Anglia
Wessex
Sussex
Kent
Gynedd
Powys
Dyfed
kingdoms
Celts

What you need and preparation

Go to your local reference library and find out about local evidence of Saxon settlement. You will also need: photocopiable pages 106–7.

What to do

15 mins Introduction

Use the map on photocopiable page 106 and the facts given in 'Background information' to talk to the children about the kingdoms of the Dark Ages and the people who shared the island at the time. The map shows the position in about the early 8th century. Make links with the present where possible. For instance, some of the names are used as modern county or regional names – Wessex is used in a royal title. Other names have changed – Kernow is still used as a Celtic version of Cornwall and Eoforwic has transformed itself into York.

Locate your own area on the map. You could also show where the invaders of that area might have come from, using the information above.

30 mins Development

Give a copy of photocopiable pages 106–7 to each group. Explain that *The Anglo-Saxon Chronicle* was a timeline written by monks in the Anglo-Saxon period. They recorded

a couple of events for each year and the things they chose to include tell us what they thought was important.

The extract from *The Anglo-Saxon Chronicle* on photocopiable page 107 gives entries between the years 681 and 704. Ask the children to read the timeline to find the places that are included on the map, and to write them down. Then help them to notice that all the entries are about fighting between kingdoms and peoples, or about the Church. They demonstrate the importance of the Church and also how violent the period was.

 Plenary

Confirm the names of the places on the map that are referred to in the timeline on page 107 and sum up the key events that are listed. Invite the children to talk about whether they would have liked to have lived in Britain during Saxon times.

Differentiation

Give adult support to less able children so that they can study the map while the timeline text is read to them. Encourage more able children to write an imaginative piece about living at that time.

Assessing learning outcomes

Can the children identify corresponding information between the map and the timeline? Can they pass a reasoned opinion about aspects of early English life?

Why is King Alfred called 'the Great'?

1 hour

Learning objectives
- Use documentary sources to identify different ways in which the past is represented.
- Learn about a significant historical character.

Lesson organisation
Class introduction followed by group work.

Vocabulary
documents
sources
contemporary

Background information

At the end of the 8th century the first Viking raids occurred on coastal areas of Britain. At first the attacks were sporadic. The raiders simply pillaged and returned home. But in 851 a Viking army stayed all winter and ravaged the south-east. In 865 another army landed near York. This time they were intent on conquering kingdoms and even settling down to farm. The Saxon kingdoms fell like dominoes – first Northumbria, then Mercia. In 870 East Anglia was attacked and its king, Edmund, was killed. The Pictish kingdom and the Welsh suffered similarly.

By 871, only Wessex was left unconquered. By great bad luck the royal house of Wessex lost four members in succession and when King Ethelred died after Easter only his younger brother Alfred was left. For the next seven years Alfred fought a largely losing battle against the 'Great Army', as the Danes were known. A surprise attack, soon after Christmas in 878, overran Wessex, and Alfred escaped with only a small band of retainers to Athelney in the Somerset wetlands. It was here that the famous episode of the burned cakes was supposed to have happened. Somehow Alfred rallied his kingdom and in early summer he met part of the Great Army under their chief, Guthrum, at Edington and won a great victory.

Alfred received the formal submission of the Danes and baptised some of the leaders. In 886 he took London and began to call himself king of England. An imaginary line was drawn across the country. The north and east was called the Danelaw and it was allowed to be under Danish influence, whilst owing allegiance to Alfred. In fact the Danes did not go away, nor did Alfred have much real power over the Danelaw.

Alfred was, however, a truly great leader. He fostered education, built up trade and commerce and laid the foundations of a united England. He was a skilled propagandist and he encouraged a monk, Asser, to write a biography of him. Asser's *Life of King Alfred* is available in full on the Internet, as is *The Anglo-Saxon Chronicle*, a timeline of English history probably first collected in his reign.

What you need and preparation

Collect together a variety of sources on Alfred the Great. The websites http://sunsite.berkeley.edu/OMACL/KingAlfred/part1.html; http://sunsite.berkeley.edu/OMACL/Anglo/part2.html have the complete text of Asser's *Life of King Alfred*. This includes a famous story about his childhood and the cakes story. The Berkeley site, http://sunsite.berkeley.edu/OMACL, also has a complete text of *The Anglo-Saxon Chronicle*, but you may prefer to obtain Anne Savage's version (Guild publishing), which has accompanying explanation and illustrations. You will also be able to find information in encyclopedias. Prepare packs of information for the children to work on in groups, making sure the sources are clearly labelled with the author and date. You will also need: board or flip chart; writing materials.

What to do

20 mins Introduction
Tell the children the story of the reign of King Alfred (871–901), drawing from the facts in 'Background information' as well as any other sources you may have access to. Explain that many people have written about Alfred both in his time and since. Show them some of the books you have collected and tell them about Asser. Explain that they will be examining a variety of accounts in groups in order to look at the different ways people have written about Alfred.

Examine one text as a whole class, to demonstrate the process. Ask one of the children to read out the text, then discuss it to make sure that everyone has understood the content. Compile a fact file which comprises notes about the source (see an example, right).

25 mins Development
Give the groups a selection of sources to examine, allocating a different source to each group. Tell the children that you would like them to read the source and then complete a 'fact file' about King Alfred.

15 mins Plenary
Invite the groups to report back to the class on their texts. Sort the texts into contemporary and later sources, and make a class timeline of the factual information gathered about Alfred's life. Some facts will be in most accounts and you can discuss how later writers must have used the Chronicle or Asser as sources. Ask the children which accounts they think are the most accurate.

Name of source

Life of King Alfred

Who wrote it?

A monk called Asser

When was it written?

About AD 880

Is it a contemporary source? (Was the writer alive at the time of the events he or she is describing?)

Yes

List of the main facts in the document:

1 Alfred learned to read so that he could win the poetry book from his mother.
2 Alfred helped his brother Ethelred fight the Danes.
3 Ethelred died and Alfred became King.
4 Alfred got told off by a cowherd's wife for letting her cakes burn.
5 Alfred won a big battle against the Danes.

Differentiation

The fact files can be compiled by mixed-ability groups but care must be taken that the less literate have clearly defined tasks. You can also differentiate by the type and number of accounts you give to the groups.

Assessing learning outcomes

Can the children use the sources to gather factual information about Alfred? Can they give reasoned opinions about the merits of the different accounts?

ICT opportunities
• Use the completed fact files to build up a database.
• Search the Internet for further information on Alfred the Great.

The Vikings

Most people use the word *Viking* to describe all people from Scandinavia in the early medieval period. Many books point out that the Vikings were not just savage raiders but traders, farmers and craftsmen. In fact, the word was used at that time precisely to mean a raider or pirate; to go *a-viking* meant to set off on a raid. Certainly it was the raiding that gave them such a prominent role in the annals of the time, and it was as raiders that they enter British history.

It is not immediately obvious why the Vikings suddenly emerged as the scourge of Europe. Culturally they were akin to the Angles, Saxons and Jutes who settled England. The Old Norse language was quite close to Anglo-Saxon and many of their customs were similar. The biggest difference between the two peoples at the time being studied was the fact that the Scandinavians were pagan and the English Christian. A second factor was their maritime skill and confidence that allowed them to cross the Atlantic in open boats. A third reason is the political situation in Scandinavia, where fairly small areas of land suitable for cultivation were supporting rather a large warrior elite. This led both to a need for sources of wealth to finance power struggles, and to groups of rootless warriors who had been exiled during those power struggles. The Vikings who came to England were mostly Danes, or under Danish leadership. In Scotland and Ireland, Norwegians were prominent.

AD793   The year of the first Viking raids. The 'heathen men' in their dragon ships came and burned the monasteries of Lindisfarne and Jarrow and terrified the recently converted Anglo-Saxons like the 'wrath of God'.

AD865   The Danish Great Army lands.

AD867   Northumbria falls to the Vikings.

AD870   East Anglia falls.

AD871   Alfred the Great is crowned king of Wessex.

AD878   The Battle of Edington. King Alfred defeated the Danes, but the Danes maintained their influence over about half the country, called the Danelaw, under the nominal overlordship of Alfred.

AD919   Viking kingdom of York (Jorvik) founded.

AD1003   Svein of Denmark invades. Svein gained the allegiance of the Danelaw and became king of half of England.

AD1016   The Battle of Ashington. Cnut of Denmark became king of all England, succeeded by Harald, then Hardicnut.

AD1042   Death of Hardicnut – Edward the Confessor becomes king. Edward was a descendent of Alfred so this was a reversion to the old English royal house.

AD1066   Edward dies.

AD1066   Norman invasion. William of Normandy was of Viking descent, so in a way this was a final Viking victory.

UNIT: The Vikings

Enquiry questions	Learning objectives	Teaching activities	Learning outcomes	Literacy links	Cross-curricular Links
When did the Vikings first come to Britain?	• Learn facts about the early Viking raids. • Consider different viewpoints of the Viking raids using the evidence of a story.	Read story of the Lindisfarne raid on pages 108–9. Use source material to draw pictures of the story and sequence them. Debate between Vikings and monks.	Children: • discuss whether the pictures show accurate representations of some aspects of monastic life and of Viking raids • use the story to discuss the two viewpoints	Write a first-person account of incidents in a story from a Viking's point of view.	Art: use pictorial sources as a basis for sketching. Explore the technique of English illuminated manuscripts.
What were Viking ships like?	• Use evidence to answer questions about Viking ships in ways that go beyond simple observations.	Teacher input about Viking ships and worksheet using evidence of the Gokstad ship.	• answer questions about Viking ships using evidence from the plan and picture on page 110	Write a first-person account of sailing on a Viking ship.	
What did the Vikings believe?	• Use documentary sources to answer questions about Viking beliefs in ways that go beyond simple observations. • Give some reasons for people's actions in past societies.	Shared reading of Ibn Fadlan's account of Viking funeral on pages 112–13. Sequence events on the board. Class discussion about reasons for Viking customs.	• answer questions using the account as evidence • put forward sensible reasons for the slave girl's actions	Write a first-person account from the point of view of the slave girl. Read other Norse myths and legends.	
Why is King Alfred called 'the Great'?	*see* Anglo-Saxons grid on page 19.				
Where did the Vikings settle?	• Use evidence from place-names to learn about Viking settlement in the local area.	Teacher-led discussion about how Viking place-names originated. Pair or group work finding Viking place-names on a local area map.	• find the Viking derivations of local place-names • understand that such people lived in their area	Label local maps with translations of Viking names.	Art: create a wall display of the area with illustrations. Geography: explain how settlements change using appropriate vocabulary and a variety of maps.
What was life like in Viking England?	• Combine information from various sources to learn about some aspects of Viking life.	Teacher-led discussion about Jorvik. Group research on aspects of Viking life. Posters produced for Viking crafts.	• put together information about Viking life from different sources	Locate information using contents pages and index, headings and so on. Read information passages and identify main points. Make a simple record of information read. Report writing on conclusions. Descriptive writing about an imaginary walk around a Viking town.	Art/design and technology: create replicas of Viking artefacts and artwork.
How did Anglo-Saxon/Viking England end?	• Use a pictorial source to find out about the Battle of Hastings. Place events in sequence.	Use the Bayeux tapestry to sequence the story of Harold, William and the Battle of Hastings. Write factual account.	• write a sequenced account of the story to accompany selected parts of the tapestry	Plot a sequence of episodes in a known story.	
Who invaded and settled in Britain long ago?	• Sequence some events and aspects of life over a long historical period.	Invasion and settlement timeline quiz.	• recall and sequence information from the topics studied.		ICT: create a database of questions on the topic.

When did the Vikings first come to Britain?

Background information

In about AD790 the first Viking raid was recorded, in Dorset. In the subsequent 150-odd years they became such a source of terror to the Christian world that they were seen as a punishment sent by God. They started with carefully planned attacks on rich targets like religious houses, attacking with great savagery and escaping quickly with plunder and slaves. By the mid-9th century, they were combining into great fleets, landing armies and holding kingdoms to ransom in a protection racket on a vast scale. Vikings founded Dublin and Kiev, Normandy and Russia. They sailed to America, settled Greenland, and were a military and political force in Constantinople.

The targets for raids seem to have been chosen on the basis of good information, which was probably gathered on trading expeditions. Traders saw richer pickings in undefended religious sites so they went home and advertised for a Viking crew. Raiders joined such a crew for the season on a contractual basis for a share in the profits. About a dozen ships might form a small fleet to make a trip in between essential work on their farm at home. The raids were quick and savage. As with more modern gangsters they relied on a violent reputation as well as a real willingness to use torture in order to get victims to hand over their treasure. The very fact that the Vikings were not afraid to steal from the Church was appalling to Christian Europe.

The attack on Lindisfarne in 793 was the first big raid in England. It was recorded in *The Anglo-Saxon Chronicle* and the opening words of the entry are at the beginning of the story on photocopiable page 108 (in bold). Lindisfarne was a religious house founded by Saint Aidan, famous for its beautiful calligraphy and illuminations. The Lindisfarne Gospels were saved from the raid along with much of the communion silver and other treasure, but some monks were abducted. We know that Emperor Charlemagne of France tried to ransom them but we do not know if he succeeded.

Some general information on the Vikings is at www.pastforward.co.uk/vikings/index.html; www.pastforward.co.uk/vikings/vikexp.html offers the visit of a 'real Viking' to your school!

What you need and preparation

Collect together pictures and resources relating to Anglo-Saxon religious life and to Viking ships, dress and weapons. There are many books for children on the Vikings, and you can find information in the English Heritage book *What do we know about the Vikings?* You can find pictures of the Lindisfarne Gospels, the sort of thing that Cuthbert (a character in the story) might have been working on, at http://www.bl.uk/diglib/treasures/lindisfarne.html. You will also need: photocopiable pages 108–9; paper; Blu-Tack; writing and drawing materials.

What to do

30 **Introduction**
Read the story on photocopiable pages 108–9 to the children. Check that they have understood the content and ask the children if they can answer the question at the foot of the photocopiable page. Establish that the people featured in the story are the monks and the Viking raiders. Then focus on two main strands: first the information given about the English monastic way of life, the importance of writing and books and of religion in general; secondly the contrast between the ferocity of the Viking raid and their commercial attitude to violence. Point out key phrases such as: *Since then my life has been a bad dream* and *They have robbed God's church and slaughtered his priests, but they behave as if it was just business.*

Refer to the pictures you have collected to clarify what the monastery and the Viking ships looked like to give the children background information.

30 mins Development

Provide the children with suitable source pictures and ask them to draw a picture illustrating a scene from the story. This could be:

- Cuthbert and Brother Oswald in the scriptorium
- the Viking ships approaching the beach
- the Vikings attacking the monks
- monks carrying away the silver cups and books to hide them
- the Viking ship at sea with oarsmen and steersman.

Or let the children draw their own chosen scene. Encourage them to give accurate detail in their pictures and to write captions using text from the story.

15 mins Plenary

Ask the children to help you to sequence a selection of their finished pictures on the board, using Blu-Tack. Pick out accurate detail for comment and re-read the corresponding sections of the story.

Differentiation

By outcome. Encourage more able children to retell the story from the point of view of a Viking.

Assessing learning outcomes

Do the children's pictures show accurate representations of some aspects of monastic life and a Viking raid? Can the children use the story to discuss the viewpoint of the Vikings and the monks?

50 mins What were Viking ships like?

Background information

We know about Viking ships both from contemporary accounts in the sagas and also from archaeology. A number of ships and boats of various types have been found in Scandinavia, and the national museums of Denmark and Sweden have done a lot of work to find out how they were constructed. This activity is based on the Gokstad ship found in Norway. It was built not long after the raid on Lindisfarne around 850. Some of the ships found were used for burials (the ship was not always burned – see the next activity); others were sunk in mud or sand, which preserved them.

The Gokstad ship had 32 oars that passed through holes in the side. There were 64 shields attached to hooks on the gunwale. This probably means that each oar had two men on it, one to row while the other rested. It had a mast that would have carried a square sail. This could only be used if the wind was blowing in the right direction, otherwise the oars would be used. The racks (shown at D on photocopiable page 110) may have been used to lay the mast on when it was not in use or more likely they could have been used to support a tent to roof the boat at certain times.

People have made reconstructions of the Gokstad ship and we know that it would have sailed fast and could survive in very rough seas because its light shallow construction allowed it to leap over the waves rather than be swamped. The sailing ability of Viking ships was greatly improved by adding a keel along the centre of the underside of the ship to reduce the rolling motion.

What you need and preparation

Find pictures of a reconstruction of a Viking ship sailing (for example, on http://www.libertynet.org/viking/pictures). You will also need: photocopiable pages 110 (an enlarged copy plus individual copies) and 111; writing materials.

The Vikings

ICT opportunities
Use the Internet to find reconstructions of Viking ships.

ICT opportunities
Use the Internet to find reconstructions of Viking ships.

What to do

10 mins Introduction
Talk about the importance of the ship in Viking raids. Ask the children for their ideas about why it was crucial for the Vikings to have ships on which they could depend. Establish that the ship enabled the Vikings to arrive and depart swiftly and safely, carrying men and booty.

30 mins Development
Now show the children the enlarged copy of photocopiable page 110 and look at the archaeology of the Viking ship. Explain that the top picture is a diagram and a bird's-eye view, while the second is an artist's impression. The first shows things that archaeologists have actually found; the second involves interpretation. Ensure that the children notice the letters and understand that they are used to refer to elements of the picture. Distribute copies of photocopiable pages 110–11 and go through the questions before asking the children to answer them. The answers are:
● The holes were for the oars.
● The hooks at B were for the shields to hang on.
● C was a hole for the mast.
● D was probably to support a tent (but discuss the children's own ideas).
● There are many possible answers to the last question – it was cold and wet because there was no cabin; it was crowded because there were so many men on it; it was exciting; it was dangerous, and so on.

10 mins Plenary
Discuss the children's answers together, particularly the last ones. Focus on the point that they have used the evidence given in the diagram and illustration on the photocopiable page to form their conclusions, but they have also had to make reasoned guesses.

Differentiation
Give less able children a selection of possible answers to choose from when they are working on the photocopiable page. Invite more able children to write a more detailed account of what it would have been like to have sailed on such a ship.

Assesing learning outcomes
Can the children answer questions using the pictures as evidence and also make conclusions based on reasoned opinion?

Follow-up activities
● Create a class Viking ship for display. Incorporate shields made by the children and make a cloth sail for a three-dimensional effect. The Vikings often treated their favourite possessions as if they were alive and gave them names that described what they did. Swords were called 'leg-biter' or 'man-slayer'; ships might be called 'swan neck' or 'fire dragon' or 'storm-rider'. Your class ship should have a suitably rousing name given by the children.
● If you have a suitable playground area, mark out the dimensions of the Gokstad ship on it using chalk (approximately 24m × 5m). The children can sit inside and get an idea of the size of the ship. Remember to point out that the Viking warriors would be big men and they would be much more cramped. Role-play a voyage, with the children rowing in unison and moving with the ship's movement on the waves. Help to set the scene by talking about the conditions – how long the men would have remained on the ship, the wind and the spray, the threat of storms, and so on.

50 mins What did the Vikings believe?

Learning objectives
● Use evidence to answer questions about Viking beliefs in ways that go beyond simple observations.
● Give reasons for people's actions in other societies.

Background information
The Vikings worshipped many different gods, but had three main ones: Odin (the chief god), Thor and Frey. They did not have any special buildings for worship, and they believed that another life awaited them when they died. This was why they were often buried with things that they thought would be useful to them in the next life. There are very few contemporary accounts of Viking religious practices. Photocopiable page 112 is based on Ibn Fadlan's description of a Viking funeral and is interesting because he was a Muslim and gives an outsider's viewpoint. The account is late (AD922) and he is talking about events in Bulgaria where he was an ambassador, but it agrees with what we know about Viking religious rituals from elsewhere.

What you need and preparation
You will need photocopiable pages 112–13; board or flip chart; writing materials.

What to do

Introduction
20 mins Read the story on photocopiable pages 112–13 to the children. When do they think it was written? Talk about the account with the class and sequence on the board the events that took place:
● dead body roofed over while preparations made
● selection of slave girl
● ship set up on the stack of wood
● food and animals put in the ship
● ceremony when the girl looks into the world of the dead
● the burning of the ship.

Discuss what the Vikings believed and why they did things this way. Mention two or three central points:
● The Vikings believed that you could take possessions with you into the world of the dead.
● They believed that you needed food for the journey.
● They were not frightened of dying and they thought that the world of the dead was a nice place to go to.

Finish by asking the children why they think the girl volunteered to die. Encourage them to make suggestions – there may be several reasons, such as:
● The girl was looking forward to being reunited with her parents and other relatives who had died.
● She also thought that she would be given the chance to see her master again, whom she was fond of.
● Maybe she was bullied into it.
● Perhaps she had a hard life anyway and thought the world of the dead would be better.

Development
20 mins Ask the children to write a first-person account of the ceremony from the point of view of the slave girl. They should focus on the moment just before she goes to join her master and include details about what has happened up to this point. Encourage them to include information about:
● how your master died
● what you thought of him
● the ceremony itself and its meaning from your point of view (did you really see your parents?)
● (most importantly) why you volunteered to die.

Plenary
10 mins Invite the children to read their first-person accounts to the rest of the class.

Differentiation
Provide less able children with a writing frame based on the questions above to enable them to write a descriptive sequenced account of the ceremony. Encourage more able children to write a poem about a Viking burial.

CHAPTER 1

The Vikings

Assessing learning outcomes

Can the children answer questions using the account as evidence? Can they put forward sensible reasons for the girl's action?

45 mins Where did the Vikings settle?

Learning objective
Use evidence from place-names to learn about Viking settlement in the local area.

Lesson organisation
Whole-class introduction followed by group work.

Vocabulary
See photocopiable page 114.

Background information

Most English place-names of Viking origin are in very specific areas like Lincolnshire, Yorkshire and Cumbria. Scotland, Ireland and Wales also have Viking names. The most common Viking suffix is *-by* which means 'a settlement'. Other common ones are *-thorpe* and *-thwaite*. The viking *-burgh* corresponds to the Anglo-Saxon *-borough*, meaning 'a royal centre'. There aren't any areas in the country where the place-names are exclusively Viking in origin; there are always Saxon or Celtic names alongside them.

What you need and preparation

Detailed maps of England; a reference book of place-names, for example AD Mills's *Oxford Dictionary of English Place-names* (OUP); board or flip chart; photocopiable page 114 (enlarged copy plus individual copies); paper; writing materials.

What to do

15 mins Introduction

Talk to the children about how Alfred beat the Danes at the Battle of Edington and about how they settled in the north and east of England. Display the map of England and write some of the Viking suffixes on the board (see photocopiable page 114). Ask the children to locate Viking towns on the map, and mark each town with a mapping pin. Grimsby, Scunthorpe, Harrogate and Scarborough are possible examples. Establish that Viking names are only found in certain areas and that this is evidence of where they settled. Give the meanings of the place-names mentioned, for example Grimsby is 'settlement founded by a man called Grim', referring to a book of place-names.

20 mins Development

Give a map of England to each group, together with a copy of photocopiable page 114. Ask the children to use the table on the photocopiable page to find Viking place-names on their map. They should make a list of the place-names on a separate sheet of paper.

10 mins Plenary

Write on the board a selection of the Viking place-names that the children have found. Display an enlarged copy of photocopiable page 114 and invite them to offer possible meanings

ICT opportunities
Compile a database of place-names which have Viking derivations.

for the place-names. Check their answers in a reference book and add the correct meaning for each word.

Differentiation

The difficulty of the activity depends largely on the map used and the number of places included. Prepare a simplified traced map showing fewer places, for less able children.

Assessing learning outcomes

Can the children find the Viking derivations of place-names and do they understand that such people really lived in the area?

Follow-up activity
Display a large pictorial map of an area of England and include information about Viking place-names. For example, draw a group of Viking cottages around the name Grimsby and add the sentence *Grim and his people lived here.*

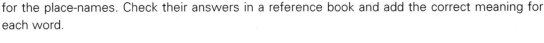

What was life like in Viking England?

1 hour

Background information

After about 30 years of raiding in England, finding plunder was getting much harder partly because everything worth having near the coast had either been stolen already or well hidden. Christian rulers were also making efforts to improve defences. The Viking response was to increase the size of the attacking force and to go in for longer campaigns.

By 850, fleets of a hundred ships, carrying large armies, were attacking whole kingdoms and building base camps to stay over the winter. Some camps like Dublin became towns in their own right. Apart from incidental plundering along the way, these armies aimed to collect vast sums of protection money in order to go away for a time. Leaders of such armies called themselves kings, though they often had no kingdom.

In 865 a great Danish army landed in East Anglia with the expressed purpose of taking over the land and settling. Over the next 14 years the Danes conquered East Anglia, Northumbria and Mercia, leaving only Wessex of all the English kingdoms. King Alfred beat them at Edington and stopped their advance, but the north and east remained under Danish domination, leaving a distinct cultural heritage. In 1013 King Sven (or Sweyn in English) conquered England. His son Cnut (Canute) reconquered and consolidated the kingdom more than any previous king. Finally, William of Normandy, descendant of Rollo, the Viking, ushered in a new age in 1066.

The differences between Viking and Anglo-Saxon culture should not be exaggerated and their settlements and farms were similar in many ways, but trade and commerce were very important to the seafaring Vikings and they were quick to develop market towns.

The old Roman city of Eboracum (York) had become the English town of Eoforwic. It was conquered by the Vikings in 866 and ruled by Danish kings until Eric Bloodaxe was driven out in 954. Extensive excavations in York have yielded a lot of information about everyday Viking life. The Jorvik Viking Centre is a favourite school visit with many. Their website is www.yorvik-viking-centre.co.uk.

Learning objectives
● Combine information from various sources.
● Learn about some aspects of Viking life.

Lesson organisation
Class introduction followed by group work on research.

Vocabulary
chiefs
warriors
slaves
weaving loom
quern
Jorvik
chess

What you need and preparation

Collect together sources of information about everyday Viking life, with pictures both of people and artefacts. The Jorvik Viking Centre information pack contains useful material which can be separated into individual information sheets easily. The British Museum have produced a Viking activity book which is well suited to Years 3 and 4, and inexpensive.

What to do

15 mins Introduction

Use the facts given in 'Background information' to talk with the children about how the Vikings settled in northern and eastern England as well as western Scotland, Wales and Ireland.

Ask the children about the different sorts of people who might have lived in a Viking town like Jorvik – chiefs, warriors, slaves and traders. Ask them to think about what sorts of things the women would do when the men were travelling to fight or trade. Talk about the sorts of crafts necessary to produce the things Vikings used.

30 mins Development

Divide the children into groups and ask each group to research a different area of Viking life. These might include:

- Viking clothes
- Viking weapons
- things you would find in a Viking house (weaving looms, querns and so on)
- Viking games (the Lewis chess set, for instance)
- Viking jewellery and decoration.

Explain that they will use their research to produce a poster. Give the children time to discuss the material they have been given and select what they think would be most useful for their topic. Members of the group can draw, trace or scan pictures before the group decides how to arrange the pictures on their poster and plan and write captions that will explain them to the rest of the class.

15 mins Plenary

Ask the groups to take it in turns to present their posters to the rest of the class. Encourage the class to formulate questions to ask the 'expert' group.

Differentiation

The research can be differentiated by the source material given, from basic copying from pictures to reading and interpreting written information. Mixed-ability groups allow for appropriate task setting.

Assessing learning outcomes

Can the children put together information from various sources about Viking life?

ICT opportunities
Compile a database of information about the Vikings.

Follow-up activities
- In an art or design and technology lesson, the children could make replicas of Viking objects.
- Prepare a Viking tableau for presentation in an assembly.

Britain and the wider world in Tudor times

The Programme of Study for Key Stage 2 leaves untouched the period between the Norman Conquest and 1485 when, with the Battle of Bosworth, Henry Tudor became King Henry VII of England. The Tudor period is the English Renaissance, a time when England became conscious of itself as a nation. The same could probably be said of Scotland, though only south of the highland line.

For nearly 100 years rival claimants to the throne from the Houses of York and Lancaster had been fighting over the succession in what was known as the Wars of the Roses. The fighting was intermittent and generally involved fairly small numbers, so much of the country was unaffected, but central authority was weak. Henry Tudor was descended from John of Gaunt through the illegitimate Beaufort line, so his claim to the throne was shaky, but he succeeded in ending the conflict and establishing himself mainly because, with Richard III dead, there was no other contender left who was strong enough to oppose him.

Henry is seen as a type of ruler typical of the Renaissance, the absolutist monarch. This means that local aristocrats like the Percys in Northumberland were no longer allowed to be petty kings in their own regions. The king was not a medieval overlord but the absolute head of a central administration. Law and money came to mean more than tradition and birth. The invention of the printing press had caused an explosion of ideas and the increased importance of the towns, and the merchant classes created a new, literate and powerful group. Henry used them in his 'Civil Service' to collect taxes efficiently, ensure that laws were obeyed, regularise trade and minimise the personal power of other individuals. He is not a great favourite for school work as his main achievements were comparative peace, stability and prosperity. This was the beginning of an intensive period of colonisation that left Europe controlling the destiny of large areas of the rest of the world. There are many reasons why this happened, but the three main ones are:

● The new European hunger for wealth and luxury goods; there was a new social mobility in Europe that came with the rise of the merchant classes. It was possible to rise from humble beginnings to positions of power, and equally possible for aristocrats to sink very low. The catalyst in each case was wealth or the lack of it. Name, family and breeding were no longer enough. The exploration of the Americas was driven by the greed for gold, silver or anything precious.

● Technological advances, particularly in the areas of maritime transport, navigation and weaponry, meant that regular long-distance communication was much more feasible.

● The explosion of ideas that came with the printing press meant that knowledge of distant places and their potential was available to many more people, Columbus was an avid reader. Renaissance philosophers were challenging ideas about the world and encouraging empirical observation.

In 1492 Columbus reached the Caribbean and opened the Americas up to European exploitation. Since he sailed under Spanish sponsorship, Spain became the richest and most powerful nation in Europe through its monopoly of trade with the New World.

In 1509 Henry VIII came to the throne as a promising and handsome young man. The first 20 years of Henry's reign were not wildly successful – he fought wars with Scotland and France and succeeded only in turning his father's budget surplus into a major deficit. He replaced his father's administrators with his own and produced a daughter, Mary. The next 20 years were dominated by the king's marital crises and England's break with the Roman Church, the two matters being closely related.

Henry was succeeded by his young son, Edward, in 1547. Edward was a child and his guardian, the Duke of Somerset, dominated him. Under this influence Edward made serious moves towards Protestantism and started to reform worship in the Church which Henry had left untouched. Catholic priests were executed, and a 'Book of Common Prayer' in English introduced.

On the death of Edward from illness in 1553, his sister, Mary Tudor, acceded to the throne (after nine days of Lady Jane Grey). Mary, like her mother, Catherine of Aragon, was a devout Catholic and pro-Spanish. She reintroduced Catholicism, and burned rather more Protestants than her brother

had burned Catholics. She married Philip II, King of Spain, and struggled hard against her advisers to get him made King of England.

In 1558 Mary was succeeded by her sister Elizabeth, daughter of the ill-fated Anne Boleyn. She reigned for 45 years and she is remembered as one of the most successful of English and British Monarchs. Her reign was characterised by sporadic conflict with Spain over two main issues, Philip of Spain's claim through marriage to the English throne and Spain's anger over continual piracy and illegal trading by English sailors like Drake and Hawkins.

Elizabeth had refused to name her successor until on her deathbed in 1603, but when she did it was her cousin, King James of Scotland, the son of Mary, whom she had executed.

The Programme of Study requires us to look at significant events and individuals, including monarchs and everyday life. The monarchs in question have helpfully left a good deal of material to use, notably the portraits that were part of a conscious effort to promote cults of personality. The increase in printing and literacy in the period means that there are also many documents. There is no requirement to cover the whole of the period, and the lesson plans provided in this chapter centre on either Henry VIII or Elizabeth.

Henry VIII

Henry was never meant to be king. His elder brother, Arthur, was the heir to the throne. It was to Arthur that Catherine of Aragon was betrothed. She was a member of the richest and most powerful royal house in Europe and she and the large dowry she brought were a great catch. When Arthur died just before the wedding, she and the money seemed too valuable to send back. Henry was 'first reserve' for the marriage and the succession, and in some ways he seems to have spent the rest of his life trying to prove that he was the real king.

Henry was handsome, wrote and played music, published religious writings, and jousted and hunted well. He was also vain and self-centred with a volcanic temper. His daughter Elizabeth was also all of these things, but there were differences. Whereas Elizabeth identified herself with England and its interests as her own, Henry identified England's interests with his own desires. Whilst many factors were in play, there is little doubt that the history of England took a decisive turn on the strength of a middle-aged man's libido. The creation of the Church of England, a hierarchical national Church ultimately in the Sovereign's control, put England in a unique position in the upheavals of the Reformation.

Strong, personalised, absolutist monarchies were a feature of the age, but Henry made his uniquely English. Despite rebellions and his cruelties, Henry managed to be more well known and popular than previous monarchs. He (despite his Welsh ancestry) advertised himself as the archetypal, robust Englishman.

Henry's marriages, which have always been a great favourite in schools, were to:
- Catherine of Aragon (King of Spain's daughter, mother of Mary Tudor – divorced)
- Anne Boleyn (mother of Elizabeth – executed for adultery, treason, witchcraft and so on)
- Jane Seymour (a submissive teenager, mother of Edward VI – died in childbirth)
- Anne of Cleves (Henry married her on the strength of an over-flattering portrait; he referred to her as 'the Flemish mare' – she was sensible, accepted a generous divorce settlement, and lived happily and as a single woman for many years)
- Katherine Howard (beautiful but not bright – executed for adultery with the servants)
- Katherine Parr (clever, cosmopolitan and politically aware; had a lot to do with Elizabeth in her youth; she survived Henry and went on to marry the love of her life, Tom Seymour).

UNIT: Henry VIII

Enquiry questions	Learning objectives	Teaching activities	Learning outcomes	Literacy links	Cross-curricular links
What was Henry VIII like?	● Use sources to answer simple questions that go beyond simple observations – draw deductions.	Look at images of Henry from young prince to old king. After recording impressions use reference books to support conclusions.	Children: ● write a paragraph: *We think Henry was… because…*	English: word portraits of Henry.	Art: portraiture and its use to create specific images.
What was the Northern Renaissance?	● Recognise characteristic features of the past and demonstrate an ability to describe some of the main changes and events.	Teacher-led discussion about the Northern Renaissance. Refer to important characters using Erasmus as an example. Define characteristics of 'Renaissance man'. Individual activity.	● identify characteristics of 'Renaissance man' and suggest why characters might fit the bill	Read some of Henry's poetry, eg 'Pastime with good company' and look at how Renaissance poetry was constructed.	Art: look at work by Holbein, Dürer and other painters of the period. Look at portraits of Erasmus and More. Were they made for the same purpose as Henry's?
What was important about *The Field of the Cloth of Gold*?	● Give reasons for and some results of main events and changes.	Read the story on pages 117–18, 'England meets France'. Look at the painting of the event. Group role-play based on story. Individual task to finish.	● explain why Henry went to France and how he hoped to impress Francis	Storyboard the visit. Poetry: shared writing on the topic of 'The Joust'.	Geography: use maps to show how Europe was controlled by different fractions. How might this lead to tension?
What was life like at court?	● Recognise characteristic features of the past. ● Select and combine information.	Structured research: children work in groups to investigate the life of Henry's court. Groups produce a poster or contribute a page to a class book detailing results of search.	● describe different aspects of court life	Describe some of the main features of life in a Tudor court, making reference to specific terms.	Music: investigate the type of music used either for processions or for dancing. PE: learn a Tudor dance such as a pavan.
What happened between Henry and Anne?	● Know that some events, people and changes have been interpreted in different ways and suggest possible reasons for this.	Look at one of Henry's love letters to Anne. What impression does this give us? How might Catherine have felt about this? In threes children role-play the situation giving the different perspectives.	● draw characters with speech bubbles giving their feelings about the situation of the divorce	English: letter writing using formal language/courtly love, with reference to Anne's letters to Henry.	Citizenship: discuss motivation and whether the end justifies the means. How much should we consider the needs of others?
What was the effect of Henry's break with Rome?	● Give some reasons for, and results of, main events and changes.	Timeline Henry's break with Rome. Pairs sequence events and discuss the effects that these produced.	● give three things that Henry achieved from the break with Rome	List pros and cons of Henry's actions.	RE: differences between Catholicism and Protestantism.
Why did Thomas More have to die?	● Know that some events, people and changes have been interpreted in different ways and suggest possible reasons for this.	Pairs activity. Research the problem that Thomas More found himself with. One child gives reasons why he should sign, the other reasons why he cannot.	● suggest reasons why Thomas More acted as he did	Describe Holbein's portrait of More's family. Shared text, *A Man for All Seasons*.	RE: investigate the concept of martyrdom; find out about the lives of martyrs both from the distant past and more modern ones.
Why was the *Mary Rose* important?	● Give some reasons for, and results of, main events and changes.	Investigate the *Mary Rose*. Look at the innovations taking place in navigation at this time and why Henry wanted to build warships.	● explain how Tudor ship-building developed and why Henry wanted to expand the navy	Create inventory for Tudor warship. Read *The Armourer's House* by Rosemary Sutcliffe.	Science/maths: developments in navigational techniques using astronomy and geometry.
What sort of monarchs were Edward VI, Lady Jane Grey and Mary Tudor?	● Identify characteristic features and use these to identify changes within and across periods.	From source material and individual research, compile a table comparing reigns.	● use a table to draw conclusions about the effectiveness of reigns.	English: make notes to compile table. Show ability to use table to present ideas.	Citizenship: look at how the line of succession works within the royal family.

What was Henry VIII like?

Background information

Henry VIII was born at Greenwich on January 28 1491. He was the second son of Henry Tudor and Elizabeth of York. He became heir to the throne on the death of his brother, Arthur. He succeeded in 1509 and ruled for 34 years. At the start of his reign Henry was only 18. He was tall, handsome and athletic, fond of hunting and dancing. He epitomised the popular image of a Renaissance prince. He was highly intelligent, composed music, spoke several languages and had written several books. He had inherited a stable and financially sound realm and therefore had plenty of money to spend in shows of wealth and pomp. He was charismatic and exciting but also pleasure loving and self-indulgent. He was autocratic, egocentric and inclined to cruelty. As his reign developed he became more despotic. He was afflicted with painful diseases and became grossly overweight. Many of these traits can be traced in his portraits.

Portraiture became increasingly important during the Renaissance. Images became realistic and people portrayed were recognisable as specific individuals. Monarchs employed court artists such as Hans Holbein the Younger and their work was used for diplomatic and political purposes. Portraits were used as part of negotiations when arranging marriages and to create and reinforce royal images. Members of court and other influential people also commissioned portraits. Often these smaller paintings were designed to be moved from room to room or house to house. They served as physical reminders of friends and family. While Henry didn't control his image as carefully as Elizabeth later did, he did use them to reinforce the impression of his power and wealth. His physical presence dominates the paintings much as he dominated his court.

Images can be downloaded from the following websites: www.royal.gov.uk/history/henry.html; www. royalinsight.gov.uk/199905/focus/fullpic2.html; www.tudorhistory.org/ – this is a very useful site with about 20 images of Henry at various stages in his life. Useful publications include *The Tudor Image* by Maurice Howard (Tate Gallery) and *A Teacher's Guide to using Portraits* by Sue Wilkinson (English Heritage).

What you need and preparation

Download off the Web a series of images of Henry VIII (enough for one between two children) or find some images in books that children can look at. You will also need: a portrait of Henry, either enlarged or on acetate for use with an OHP (one of Holbein's would be most appropriate as these are often the most detailed); a variety of Tudor reference books; photocopiable page 115; board or flip chart; writing materials; samples of rich fabrics (optional).

What to do

Introduction

20 mins Show the children your selected image of Henry VIII and give them a few minutes to look at the painting. Direct them to look at his clothes, expression, posture, the background and setting. Ask them what sort of person they think he is, what his character is like, and encourage them to justify their answers with specific reference to the painting. (For example, *I think he is rich because he has lots of jewels; he looks serious as he is not smiling.*) Point out specific details in the painting such as:

● Costume – look at the richness of the clothing. Silk came from China and was fantastically expensive to import as it took years for merchants to bring it overland. Bright or deep colours indicate expensive dyes. Rich fabrics such as velvet, satin and fur were also signs of wealth. (You may want to have some examples of these fabrics for children to see and feel.)

● Jewellery – how much jewellery is there and what is it like?

- Accessories/setting – is he holding or wearing anything else (for example, gloves, a sword)? Why might these have been included and what do they symbolise? What is included in the background (if there is one)? Why has this been included? (Tell the children that everything within the painting has been included on purpose; there is no incidental information, as in a photograph.)
- Pose – how is the king standing or sitting? How much of the painting does he take up?
  Collate the children's ideas on the board.

30 mins Development
Divide the children into pairs to investigate other paintings of Henry to try to find out more about what he was like. Give each pair a painting and a copy of photocopiable page 115. Explain that each child in the pair must contribute three words to describe Henry, for example *powerful*, *rich* and *important*. Together the children should then list the evidence they have found to support their viewpoint, such as *He takes up the whole picture; he is wearing jewellery; his clothes look expensive.* They can then write a joint sentence to summarise their view of what Henry was like.

Once they have completed this part of the page they should select a reference book to see what else they can find out about Henry (see 'Differentiation'). Tell the children whether they need to answer question A or B; they do not need to do both.

10 mins Plenary
Working together as a whole class, see if the children can put the pictures into chronological order:
- Has anyone got a picture of Henry as a child or a young man?
- What about as an old man?
Try to slot the other pictures into order, to form a timeline. Collate some of the information that the children have gathered by completing the statement *Henry was…*

Display the timeline of pictures and the children's comments.

Differentiation
Ask more able children to use a reference book to find out two more things about Henry. Less able children can use a reference book to find out something that substantiates their ideas about Henry.

Assessing learning outcomes
Can the children use sources to make deductions about Henry, such as *We think Henry was… because…?*

ICT opportunities
- Use *Hyperstudio* to create a stack about Henry VIII.
- Scan in the pictures the children looked at; use hidden buttons to uncover clues about Henry and use other buttons to take children on to information on other cards. (This can be developed throughout the unit of work.)

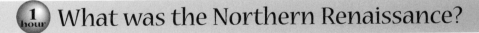

1 hour What was the Northern Renaissance?

Background information
The Renaissance started in Italy in the 14th century as scholars began to rediscover some of the ideas and achievements of the Ancient Greeks and Romans. These included philosophy, art and architecture, mathematics and engineering and literature. The writings of classical scholars were gathered together in seats of learning such as Padua and Bologna. Valuable Greek and Latin manuscripts were collected and ideas began to be disseminated throughout Europe. The 'New Learning' was characterised by a movement away from a belief in the authority of the Church to a focus on the right of the individual to effect their own salvation. In the north of Europe a group of influential scholars shared ideas and opinions through the exchange of letters and in their meetings. They gave each other paintings of themselves as tokens of their regard. One of the most important figures was the writer and philosopher Erasmus of Rotterdam. He had visited England and had

Learning objective
Recognise characteristic features of a period and demonstrate an ability to describe some of the main changes, events and people.

Henry VIII

Vocabulary
philosopher
Renaissance
writer
artist
scholar
classical period
affluent
fashionable
realistic

many friends in the country such as Sir Thomas More, the Lord Chancellor, and Hans Holbein, the painter. Henry himself had asked Erasmus to return and live in his court. The Northern Renaissance saw a flowering of the arts that was reflected in the concept of the 'cultured' individual. This person was well aware of classical ideas and learning, fluent in several languages, athletic and proficient in the creative arts.

What you need and preparation

Prepare a timeline with labels and/or pictures to mark the classical periods of Ancient Greece, the Romans and the Tudors. You will also need: a map of Europe (this needs to be large enough for children to see the detail and you should be able to write on it – you could use a large waxed cloth map or have one that has been transferred onto acetate); a large picture of Erasmus (the Metsys portrait of 1517 of Erasmus in his study is particularly appropriate); pictures of More and Holbein (optional); reference books; the Venetian ambassador's comments on Henry (see http://www.newman.ac.uk/–c.s.sutton/page3.html or *English Historical Documents*, Volume 5, edited by CH Williams, Eyre Spottiswode); photocopiable page 116; removable sticky labels; writing materials.

What to do

30 mins Introduction

Explain to the children that this session will introduce one of the important ideas relating to the Tudor period. Explain the term 'Renaissance'. What did this mean? (Rebirth.) What did it entail? (Rediscovery of ideas from the past.) What 'past' are we thinking of? Use the timeline to slot in the different classical periods.

The children may already have studied one or both of these periods. If they have, ask them what some of the most important achievements of these times were. Establish that these were:
- Greeks – medicine, literature, architecture, sculpture
- Romans – engineering, literature, architecture, organisation of an empire.

Now show the children a map of Europe. Point out Athens and Rome, marking them clearly with removable labels. Where in Europe might we expect the Renaissance to start? Where might there be visible evidence of the past?

Explain the importance of the Roman Catholic Church at this time, which:
- controlled what people thought – many except those within Church society were illiterate
- was immensely wealthy, owning and controlling vast areas of land
- had its centre situated in Rome, in its own city
- was the only religion in England at this time, rather than there being many, as now.

If we link the physical evidence and location of the Church, where could we now expect the Renaissance to begin? Ask the children to select an area. Explain that the Renaissance started in Italy and spread slowly through the rest of Europe. Plot this on the map.

Ask the children why it spread slowly. Ask them how we spread ideas and news nowadays. They may suggest that this is done through the Internet, television, radio and newspapers. As none of this was available to the Tudors, how do the children think ideas might have been spread? (Books, letters and word of mouth – news spread very slowly.)

One major innovation that helped the spread of ideas at this time was the invention of the printing press. This allowed books to be printed rather than laboriously being written out by hand. New schools and universities also helped disseminate ideas.

What was special about these ideas? Bring out the following points:
- Mankind became the focus of philosophy. People were free to ask questions about the quality of their lives and to seek their own answers rather than waiting to be told what to do by the Church.
- The human form was represented in a realistic manner, with perspective and detail in art and an understanding of anatomy in sculpture – individuals became recognisable in portraits.

- More literature was either written in or translated into the language of the country rather than Latin. This meant more ordinary people could understand it.
- People were joined by shared ideas rather than nationality.

⏱ 25 mins Development

Show the children the portrait of Erasmus. What do they think this picture tells us is important? (Learning, as demonstrated by a variety of books; correspondence with a wide circle of friends.) Erasmus was a perfect example of a 'Renaissance man' – educated, open to new ideas, 'cultured'. He had many links with England through Thomas More and Holbein, to name two of the most influential. Show pictures of these people, if possible, and explain how they were linked by their friendship.

Give the children a copy of the Venetian Ambassador's comments about Henry VIII to read. Can they decide whether Henry fitted into the idea of a Renaissance prince or not? Distribute copies of photocopiable page 116, for them to complete. Explain that for the first part they should try to identify the features that describe a Renaissance person; for the second part they should justify their answers.

⏱ 5 mins Plenary

Select two or three children to explain their answers to photocopiable page 116.

Differentiation

Provide a simplified text based on the Venetain Ambassador's comments, and adult support for less able children. Invite more able children to research one of the other influential figures of the period, for example Hans Holbein, Sir Thomas More, Dürer, and then see if they conform to the definition of a Renaissance character.

Assessing learning outcomes

Can the children understand what is meant by the term 'Renaissance'? Can they explain why certain characters could be described as epitomising the Renaissance?

ICT opportunities
- Research characters such as More, Holbein, Dürer and Metsys on the Internet.
- Make a class book about the Northern Renaissance, including examples of literature and art. Show how the characters were linked.

⏱ 1 hour What was important about *The Field of the Cloth of Gold?*

Background information

Much of the beginning of Henry's reign was spent jockeying for influence in Europe. Henry undertook campaigns against the Scots and the French and was continually involved in negotiating treaties with Spain and the Holy Roman Empire. Henry and his main adviser, Thomas Wolsey, attempted to form alliances first with Francis I of France then Charles V of HRE and then Francis once more. In May 1520 Henry decided to form a new English–French alliance. In June he journeyed to France to cement relations with Francis and to impress his own importance and power upon the French monarch.

Henry, Catherine and 5000 attendants, including almost all England's nobility, travelled to the north of France to meet the 'ancient enemy'. Henry transported vast amounts of luxury goods with which to dazzle Francis. Hundreds of tents and pavilions with huge amounts of food and drink were transported across the Channel. The bulk of these goods, including hundreds of pounds worth of velvet, satin, cloth of gold, doublets, bonnets and boots, was carried in a fleet of ships that stretched for 32 kilometres (20 miles)!

The kings met in the Val d'Or (Valley of Gold) and advanced towards each other. After they greeted each other a grand tournament commenced. Feats of strength and skill allowed the nobility

Learning objective
Give reasons for and some results of main events and changes.

Henry VIII

Lesson organisation
Whole-class discussion; group activity; individual follow-up.

Vocabulary
monarch
pavilion
cloth of gold
nobility
treasure
peasants
trumpets
sackbuts
banquet
joust
wrestling
formalities
exuberant
brocade
charger
tension
ranks
embrace
procession
throng
squire
feats of arms
prowess

to demonstrate their prowess, although there was some dismay when Francis threw Henry in a wrestling match! Vast quantities of food and drink were consumed and peasants came from miles around to drink the wine that flowed out of the fountains. Henry feasted in an enormous pavilion of cloth of gold that shone radiantly in the summer sunlight and dominated the countryside. There were banquets and dances for the nobility that culminated in the joint participation of a solemn High Mass. Promises of eternal brotherhood were sworn by the two monarchs before they parted. An obscene amount of wealth was squandered for no real purpose, however. Less than two years later, Henry concluded an alliance with Charles V and by August was at war once more with France.

For further information see: *Tudors and Stuarts* by Paul Noble (Collins *Primary History* series), *A World of Change (Britain in the Early Modern Age, 1450–1700)* by Rosemary Kelly (Stanley Thornes), www.orkan.4mg.com/HenryVIII/Chapter2.html (this has a good account of the encounter), www.bartleby.com/213/1501.html (some primary material from Edward Hall, contemporary chronicler).

What you need and preparation

Obtain a map of Europe and mark in zones of influence for France, Spain and England; remember that England still had Calais at this time and much of the Netherlands were under Spanish control (see the book *A World of Change*). Find pictures of the painting *The Field of the Cloth of Gold* (in Noble's *Tudors and Stuarts*, for example). You will also need: photocopiable pages 117–18; blank storyboard sheets (each sheet with four boxes); paper; writing materials.

What to do

20 mins **Introduction**

Give out copies of photocopiable pages 117–18 and read 'England meets France' to the children, encouraging them to follow the story on their copies. Highlight specific and unknown vocabulary such as *pavilion, peasants* and *sackbuts*. Allow time for the children to ask any questions they might have about the text. What impression of the spectacle do they get from the story? (Ensure that they justify their answers with reference to the text.) Pick out any words that relate to wealth such as *jewels, treasure, satin* and so on. What sorts of sounds would the children expect to hear if they had been present? What about smells and colours? Encourage the children to flesh out the story and to try to visualise the scene.

Ask the children:
● What was the importance of this meeting? (They met as friends rather than enemies.)
● What was Henry attempting to do with this display of wealth? (He was trying to be seen to be more successful than Francis.)

Use the map to show how different countries had influence in different parts of Europe and ask:
● Where is England?
● Where is Scotland?

Ensure that the children understand that Scotland was a separate country at this time and one which had closer links with France than with England.
● Where is France and how might this affect England?
● What areas did Spain control?

Use these questions to help the children understand about the balance of power and how this made Henry feel insecure.

20 mins **Development**

Give out a copy of the painting *The Field of the Cloth of Gold* to each group. Explain that this

is a narrative painting, and make the following points:

- The painting is made to tell a story and was painted after the event.
- People may be shown in several places at once, for example Henry is shown arriving in procession at the lower left-hand side, and greeting Francis in the pavilion to the centre of the painting.
- Enormous detail is shown to build up a picture of what was happening.
- There may well be symbolic or mythical elements, such as the dragon in the top left-hand corner (this represented the firework display that was part of the entertainment).
- Perspective was sometimes arbitrary – compare Henry with the size of the castle walls.

Discuss the different elements that can be seen in the picture. What can the children see happening?

Now ask the children to take turns to describe different scenes from the painting to the rest of their group or to their partner (circulate and direct discussion within different groups) or to relate what they see in the picture to incidents in the story (encourage them to justify their answers: *I think… because…*).

Alternatively, ask the children to work in their groups, taking one section of the painting and producing a role-play or living picture of the scene.

20 mins Plenary

Give out the blank storyboard sheets and ask the children to use the story and the picture to select four different incidents. These should be chosen to show how Henry and Francis tried to impress each other. The children should also complete the following statements, writing down their answers:

- *Henry went to France because…*
- *Henry tried to impress Francis because…*

Discuss some of the ways in which the children have finished the sentences.

Differentiation

The storyboards can be completed with differing degrees of complexity:

- lower-ability groups – mainly pictures of scenes with simple captions
- average-ability groups – storyboard pictures with sentences to explain the illustrations
- higher-ability groups – a paragraph for each scene with simple illustrations.

Assessing learning outcomes

Can the children explain why Henry went to France and how he hoped to impress Francis?

1 hour What happened between Henry and Anne?

Background information

Henry became next in line to inherit both the throne and his brother's wife when Arthur died unexpectedly in April 1502. In April 1509 Henry was crowned king and on June 11th of the same year married Arthur's widow, the Spanish princess, Catherine of Aragon. They were jointly crowned 13 days later. Through Catherine Henry gained connections with the thrones of Spain and the Holy Roman Empire which was to help shape his foreign policy in the early years. Catherine was older than Henry, with a compassionate and devout nature. The learned queen was popular and respected, with some powerful supporters on the Continent. While Henry engaged in hostilities with the French and Scots, Catherine acted as Henry's regent. For 20 years Catherine and Henry lived in relative harmony. While Henry amused himself with a succession of mistresses none proved to be a serious rival for Catherine's position. By 1527, however, things were changing. Catherine was

ICT opportunities
Ask the children to work on a desktop publishing project in groups. Invite each child in the group to contribute an article detailing the meeting of the two monarchs and what took place during the festivities. Scan in the children's own portraits of the two kings and/or illustrations of entertainment.

Learning objective
Know that some events, people and changes have been interpreted in different ways and suggest possible reasons for this.

Henry VIII

Lesson organisation
Whole-class discussion followed by individual research task and then whole-class plenary.

Vocabulary
courtly love
divorce
annulment
married
Pope
chancellor

unlikely to give birth again and although she had borne many children only the serious eleven-year-old Mary had survived.

At this point Henry encountered Anne Boleyn, sister of one of his previous mistresses and lady-in-waiting to his wife. Anne was vivacious, witty and recently returned from the sophisticated French court. Although not conventionally beautiful she was intriguing and mysterious. Henry was instantly captivated by her and fell deeply in love with her. Anne was very astute and ambitious. She was not prepared to become merely another royal mistress and held out for marriage. Henry gave Thomas Wolsey the task of obtaining a papal decree that would allow him to divorce Catherine. There were several problems with this:

● Henry had had special dispensation from a previous Pope to marry Catherine. The current Pope was loath to admit that his predecessor had made a mistake.

● Charles V, Catherine's nephew, held the Pope prisoner after attacking and sacking Rome and was fiercely opposed to a divorce, which he saw as an insult to his aunt.

● Catherine herself resolutely refused to agree to a divorce or to retire to a nunnery!

The problem dragged on for two years without any sign of providing the solution that Henry wanted. Catherine was separated from her daughter and banished. When Wolsey proved unable to procure a divorce his fate was sealed, and he was arrested but died before he could be executed. Catherine's supporters such as Sir Thomas More and Bishop John Fisher were executed for their steadfast refusal to accede to Henry's wishes. Henry's new advisers, Thomas Cromwell and Thomas Cramner, encouraged him to cut his ties with the papacy and take control of the Church himself. The stage was set for the Reformation and the creation of the Church of England.

More information can be found on: www.royal.gov.uk/history/henry.html; www.newman.ac.uk/–c.s.sutton/page3.html; www.tudorhistory.org/.

What you need and preparation

Select one of Henry's love letters to Anne (one that is not too obscure or too explicit) – this activity is based on a letter in which Henry thanks Anne for a gift of a jewelled damsel on a ship, and it can be found in *English Historical Documents*, Volume 5 edited by CH Williams (Eyre Spottiswode). You will also need: pictures of Henry, Anne, Catherine and Wolsey; speech bubbles; a selection of reference books, CD-ROM encyclopedia and database; photocopiable page 119; board or flip chart; writing materials.

What to do

15 mins **Introduction**

Read Henry's letter to Anne. You will need to read this slowly as the syntax is not always easy to understand. Explain some of the more complex vocabulary. Ask the children what type of letter it is. Ensure that they refer to the text of the letter to support their answers. Points to note include:

● Henry usually used a secretary to write his letters for him, even those that were quite intimate. Henry wrote this letter to Anne himself, however.

● Henry and Anne exchanged gifts that were symbolic as well as practical demonstrations of their affection. The lonely damsel in the ship tossed on the rough sea represented Anne beset with troubles in the court, buffeted by the different fractions trying to control her.

- Henry's letters employed the language of courtly love, with Henry talking in the third person rather than the first person.
- The original letters may well have been written in French rather than English as with the final signature, *H. autre ne cherche R.*
- Anne's letters were stolen from her probably on the orders of the Pope. The originals are kept in the Vatican archives.

Now ask the children:

- How do we know what type of letter this is?
- What does this say about these two people?
- Should Henry be sending letters like this to Anne? If not, why not?

You may need to suggest that it is not right for Henry to be sending love letters to someone else while he is still married.

- How might Catherine feel if she knew what was going on?
- What could be the solution to this problem?

Allow the children to suggest possible solutions and collate their answers on the board. Explain why some of the possibilities were not viable at that time, for example to divorce, Henry needed the permission of the Pope.

30 mins Development

Explain that the children are going to work in groups of four to research what happened in Henry's 'Great Matter'. Each will take a different character affected by the problem (Henry, Catherine, Anne and Wolsey). Tell the children that they will need to use reference books, CD-ROMs and the Internet to gather information about their character and their place in the story. They will also need to consider the character's motivation and how they felt about the situation.

Distribute copies of photocopiable page 119, which the children should use to record their research findings.

15 mins Plenary

Gather the children together with the results of their research. Display the images of the four characters. Ask the children to suggest what the characters might have to say about the situation, for example:

HENRY: *I'm in love with Anne and want to marry her.* Or:

HENRY: *I should not have married Catherine because she was my brother's wife first. God was not pleased and that is why so many of our babies died.*

Write out some of their suggestions on the speech bubbles and place them around the picture of the character concerned.

Differentiation

Provide adult support for less able groups, and simplified texts or reference books.

Assessing learning outcomes

Can the children recognise why different characters will have different views about the same event? (Do they suggest different points of view to put in the speech bubbles for the different protagonists?)

Follow-up activities

- Set the children a homework task of researching Henry's wives and children, then create a class book with the results of the research. Include information on why Henry married his wives and what happened to them.
- Make a timeline and family tree which gives facts about Henry's wives and children.

ICT opportunities

- Word-process the text for the speech bubbles, using appropriate fonts, and add them to a display of the characters, adding small clip-art illustrations.
- Encourage the children to use the Internet, where possible, for the homework research task and word-process the results.

① Why did Thomas More have to die?

Learning objective
Know that events, people and changes have been interpreted in different ways and suggest possible reasons for this.

Lesson organisation
Investigative pairs activity followed by whole-class discussion; group debate followed by whole-class plenary.

Vocabulary
Oath of Supremacy
Act of Succession
arrested
traitor
executed
tried
allegiance

Background information

Sir Thomas More was born in London in 1478, the son of Sir John More, a prominent judge. He was educated in London until going to Oxford, where he studied under some of the foremost scholars of the early Northern Renaissance, Thomas Linancre and William Grocyn. Thomas proved himself to be an eager and able student and began a lifetime of study. He became a barrister in 1501 but was also very attracted to the monastic life. While he did not become a monk he retained habits of prayer, fasting and penance all his life. He decided eventually to serve his country through the field of politics and entered Parliament in 1504. He also continued to serve as a just and impartial judge and earned increasing honours and royal favour for the work that he did. He was made Lord Chancellor after Wolsey's fall from power. He served as an important member of the court circle and of life in London. He and Erasmus were lifelong friends and he corresponded with many of the great philosophers on the Continent. For several years he and Henry were also friends, although More had no doubt of the nature of that friendship. He once remarked to the Duke of Norfolk that if his head would bring Henry one single castle in France he knew that he would lose that head! Thomas More lived a rich and fulfilling family life in a mansion on the river at Chelsea surrounded by his affectionate daughters and their families. Here in his light-filled study surrounded by his books, More wrote *Utopia*, the blueprint for the perfect city.

Thomas More was a man of high principles who was prepared to stand by his convictions. When Henry divorced Catherine of Aragon to marry Anne Boleyn, More left the king in no doubt of his feelings about the situation. More resigned as Chancellor and refused to go to Anne's coronation. When Henry tried to get him to swear to the Act of Succession (to legitimise the children of Henry and Anne) and the Oath of Supremacy (confirming Henry as supreme head of the Church of England) in 1534, he refused. He was arrested and imprisoned in the Tower of London. He was kept in the Tower for over a year before being tried and found guilty of treason. He was beheaded on July 6 1535. His head was exposed on London Bridge for a month before his daughter Margaret managed to obtain it.

More information can be found in: *Holbein and the Court of Henry VIII*, the Queen's Gallery, Buckingham Palace (Lund Humphries) – information about the More family portrait; *Tudors and Stuarts* by Paul Noble (Collins *Primary History* series); *A World of Change (Britain in the Early Modern Age 1450–1700)* by Rosemary Kelly (Stanley Thornes). www.luminarium.org/renlit/moremore.html gives a very wide range of linked sites, all related to Sir Thomas More.

What you need and preparation

Find copies of the More family portrait by Hans Holbein – these can be downloaded from the above website (you will need enough for one between two children). You will also need: a description of Thomas More by Erasmus, downloaded from the above website (optional); photocopiable page 120; pictures of Henry and Sir Thomas More – these can be downloaded from the website www.tudorhistory.org/; board or flip chart; writing materials.

What to do

⏱ 20 mins Introduction

Split the children into pairs and give them a copy of the More family portrait by Holbein. Ask them to see what they can find out about this family from their investigation of the portrait. Who is the most important person and how do they know this? Circulate, and stimulate discussion. Points to consider include:

● Setting – notice the flowers (some of these were exotic blooms from the Continent and were

therefore a symbol of wealth), the glass windows (glass was expensive at this time; it also shows how important light was for studying), the clock (a new, very high-tech feature – expensive and demonstrates an interest in science).

● Costume – rich materials, jewellery, chain of office, bright dyes, fur – all denote wealth.

● Animals – dogs and monkey show the importance of the pets to the family and also show wealth.

● Books and scrolls – evidence of learning everywhere including the fact that the women hold books. This demonstrates the importance of books and learning for this family.

Each pair of children should note down five things they have discovered and the evidence in the picture that supports their ideas.

30 mins Development

Bring the children back together and discuss what they have discovered. Collate some of their answers on the board.

Give the children a short biography of Thomas More showing his place in the court of Henry. Explain what sort of person he was (see 'Background information'). You can use some of Erasmus's description of More here, if available. Include the following points:

● Thomas More was not keen to involve himself in the intrigues of court life.

● While he was always a true friend, if he felt that someone was not honest he would try to withdraw gradually from the friendship rather than have a major argument.

● He worked hard on behalf of others rather than himself.

● He was not prepared to follow the opinions of the crowd but made up his own mind.

● He had once thought of becoming a monk.

Explain the situation that More found himself in over the question of Henry's divorce and the break with Rome. Use some of the points above to explain why he was in a quandary (he held deep religious convictions as is shown by his desire to become a monk) and how he dealt with it (he tried to withdraw from court rather than confront Henry directly). Thomas More had two alternatives:

● to hold to his convictions, refuse to swear the required oath and face the consequences – execution

● to forget his convictions and save himself by following the example of the majority of the court.

Split the class into either Group A (Henry VIII) or Group B (Thomas More). You may want to have two large groups or several smaller ones (for example, three As and three Bs) depending on the size and composition of your class. Either designate a scribe and a spokesperson for each group or allow the children to select these themselves.

Give each group a copy of photocopiable page 120 and explain that they have to put forward two or three reasons to support their point of view. All should be involved in the discussion (for which you should allow ten minutes) before the children select and justify their two or three ideas. The scribe should then record their ideas.

10 mins Plenary

Draw the children together. Allow each spokesperson to put forward the ideas for their group. Collate the ideas on two large sheets of paper headed with either a picture of Henry or Thomas More.

Encourage the children to draw some sort of conclusion about Thomas More's death:

● Was he right to behave as he did?

● What about Henry's point of view?

● Did Thomas More have to die?

● Why did he have to die?

ICT opportunities
Use the Internet to research other men and women of conscience who have stood up for something they believe in, such as Gandhi, Edith Cavell, Martin Luther King, Emily Davison. Or focus on others who were executed for their religious beliefs during this period, for example Latimer and Ridley, Bishop John Fisher. Look at both Catholic and Protestant martyrs.

Henry VIII

Follow-up activity
Prepare a class assembly on the theme of Thomas More.

Differentiation

Provide adult support for less able children and those who need help with the organisation of their group work.

Assessing learning outcomes

Can the children suggest why Thomas More acted as he did?

⟨50 mins⟩ Why was the *Mary Rose* important?

Learning objective
Give some reasons for and results of main events and changes.

Lesson organisation
Whole class; group investigation; plenary.

Vocabulary
navy
navigation
warship
gunports
canon
bronze
iron

Background information

When Henry inherited the throne, France and Scotland both threatened England with their powerful navies. England only had around five warships at this time! Henry immediately began to build up his naval capacity. In 1510 he spent £700 commissioning two warships. The smaller ship, at 300 tons, was the *Peter Pomegranate*. The larger vessel of 400 tons was the *Mary Rose*. The ship was named after Henry's sister, Mary, and the Tudor Rose, symbol of the new dynasty. It is ironic that the *Mary Rose* was to spend most of her life fighting the French, while Mary herself married the French king.

The ships were constructed in Plymouth from well-seasoned oak and elm. In 1511 the ships sailed up to London to be fitted with their guns. The *Mary Rose* was armed with heavy bronze and iron cannon. She had new watertight gunports that allowed her to carry more heavy guns lower down in the hull. This made her more stable than other ships of the time. The *Mary Rose* was state of the art at the time of her construction. Once fully laden, the ship weighed 500 tons and carried a crew of around 200 (about 185 sailors and 30 gunners). Most were young men with a few boys also in the crew. The *Mary Rose* spent her working life patrolling the coasts of England, fighting the French and Scots.

In 1545 a vast fleet was gathered by the French and sent towards Portsmouth. The French had 200 ships to the 80 English ships. Henry was personally involved in supervising the battle from the shore. The French were foiled in their invasion attempts by the extensive fortifications of Portsmouth harbour. At dawn on the 19th July, the French started firing at the English fleet who were becalmed in the harbour. Suddenly the wind got up and the English ships set sail. To the horror of all those watching on the shore, the *Mary Rose*, flagship of the fleet and Henry's delight, suddenly capsized and sank with the loss of almost all her crew. Although Henry tried to salvage her, the *Mary Rose* lay on the seabed until the 20th century.

The official website for the *Mary Rose* is www.maryrose.org/ – it includes information on the history of the ship, what life was like for different members of the crew and a database of artefacts. It is also possible to purchase a wide variety of educational resources either online or through mail order. Other information can be found in *Tudor Warship – What happened here?* by Elizabeth Newberry (A & C Black), *Mary Rose: the anatomy of a Tudor warship 1510–1988* (CSH Ltd), *What do we know about the Tudors and Stuarts* by Richard Tames (Simon & Schuster), *Tudor People* by John Fines (Batsford), *Exploration* by Tony Triggs (Wayland), *Investigating the Tudors* by Alison Honey (National Trust), *English Historical Documents*, Volume 5 edited by CH Williams (Eyre Spottiswode).

What you need and preparation

Find a picture of a Tudor warship – one of the *Mary Rose* would be ideal. You will also need: a selection of reference books; information downloaded from the Web (see above for sources); a map of the British Isles and Northern Europe, marked with the following locations: Brest, St Malo, Boulogne, Calais, Paris, Antwerp, Edinburgh, London, Plymouth and Portsmouth (a small example

of a map like this can be found on the *Mary Rose* website); board or flip chart; photocopiable page 121; writing materials.

What to do

Introduction

15 mins Discuss the main forms of transport in Tudor times. Ask the children how people moved from place to place. Establish that people went on foot or for longer distances used horses, river boats and ships. Talk about what was being imported and exported. Wool was the main trade item. How do the children think that the wool reached the Continent from England? Ensure that the children understand that the only way was by sea across the Channel.

What sort of relations did England have with her neighbours? Remind the children about *The Field of the Cloth of Gold* (see page 43). At this stage England and Henry were often at war with 'the Auld Alliance' – France and Scotland.

Show the children France and Scotland on the map. Point out that these two countries had considerable navies at the time Henry became king but that England only had a small number of ships. Ask the children what they would do if they were in Henry's position with a very small number of warships to protect his shores, some fierce neighbours who wanted to attack or invade him and a vital trade item that needed to be shipped overseas.

Collate the children's answers on the board, the main response that you are looking for being that Henry needed to get more warships. Ask the children what they think Tudor warships looked like. (You may have some children who think that they look like something out of World War II – that is, grey metal with huge guns and maybe even aircraft!)

Show the children a picture of a Tudor warship. Ask them:
● How was the ship powered – how did it move?
● Where were the armaments?
● Where did sailors live when they were on the ship?
● How was the ship steered?

Let the children look at the picture closely to suggest answers to the questions. Tell them that one of the first ships that Henry built was the *Mary Rose*.

Development

25 mins Divide the children into groups and distribute the resources you have collected, together with a copy of photocopiable page 121. Explain that they must use the sources to find out what the *Mary Rose* was like and why it was important. The group should work together and record their findings in the form of a poster, using the photocopiable page for guidance.

Plenary

10 mins Gather the children back together and invite each group to explain their poster to the rest of the class.

Differentiation

Organise the children into mixed-ability groups, and provide adult support where available.

Assessing learning outcomes

Can the children explain why the *Mary Rose* was important to Henry's foreign policy?

ICT opportunities
Use the *Mary Rose* website to research the lives of the different characters on board.

The Elizabethan age

Queen Elizabeth has caught the imagination of succeeding generations in a unique way – because she was a woman, because she reigned for a long time, because she was a remarkably talented monarch but probably most of all because she presided over the height of the Renaissance in England.

Elizabeth herself was a true Renaissance person; children will be impressed by examples of her handwriting at the age of five or six. As a child she translated books from about six languages. She often impressed ambassadors by speaking to them perfectly in their own tongues. She was an accomplished musician and voracious reader, well up to date with current ideas. She had a terrifying time during Mary's reign, and only her brilliant instincts and native caution saved her life. She was single-minded about staying in control, which she achieved by refusing to marry, playing her advisers off against one another, and using her masterly ability to leave decisions hanging in the air until the winning side became obvious.

Like her grandfather Henry VII, Elizabeth was a great judge of a good civil servant. The Cecils, father and son, served her throughout her reign, and created an efficient administration. Sir Francis Walsingham ran her 'secret police', mainly directed against Catholic supporters of Philip of Spain's claim to the throne.

There is a wealth of excellent material for the study of Elizabethan life; Shakespeare is one of the 'greats' in the history of the English-speaking world and children should know something about him. Elizabethan portraits show expressive faces and lots of objects around the figure, which give clues about the sitters. The wealthy of Elizabethan times built stately homes that are still standing. There is a reconstruction of the Globe theatre on Bankside, and the National Portrait Gallery has reproductions of Tudor portraits. Hampton Court and Hever Castle are both well worth a visit.

Spain, by backing Columbus, had laid claim to the fabulous wealth of Mexico and Peru. The vision of the New World ripe for plucking by resourceful and gallant gentlemen had a magical hold on Elizabethan seamen like Drake, Ralegh and Hawkins. They achieved extraordinary feats in search of the gold of 'Eldorado'.

In 1588 Philip of Spain launched a fleet, the famous Armada, against England. It was beaten by a combination of the weather and the skilful seamanship of Lord Howard and Drake. This year saw the height of Elizabeth's popularity and the official rise of England from minor backwater to major European state.

UNIT: The Elizabethan age

Enquiry questions	Learning objectives	Teaching activities	Learning outcomes	Literacy links	Cross-curricular links
What was Queen Elizabeth I like?	● Use sources to answer simple questions that go beyond simple observations – draw deductions.	Look at a series of images of Elizabeth from young princess to old queen. After recording impressions use reference books to support conclusions.	Children: ● use the portraits to answer questions, going beyond simple observations to draw deductions	Write character sketches focusing on details to evoke sympathy or dislike.	Art: portraiture and its use to create specific images.
How did Queen Elizabeth meet her people?	● Learn about how Elizabeth went on a royal progress and demonstrate knowledge of some aspects of Elizabethan life.	Read pages 122–3 about the royal progress. Children use facts and figures to draw or write about it.	● write an account that incorporates period detail and is consistent with historical evidence	Write independently, linking own experiences to situations in historical stories.	
What was the Elizabethan countryside like?	● Use primary and secondary sources to gather information about aspects of life in the Elizabethan countryside.	Use part of Thomas Tusser's poem on page 124 to find out about the Elizabethan farming year. Use local souces to find out about their area.	● translate Tusser; find and use appropriate reference for their illustrations	Put verse into modern prose. Identify different types of text.	Science: grow plants from Elizabethan era.
What was Elizabethan London like?	● Use primary and secondary sources to gather information about aspects of life in Tudor London.	Use map on page 125 to explore Elizabethan London. Use pictures to make a wall map.	● include accurate information from the map and film in their stories	Write independently, linking own experiences to situations in historical stories.	Geography: use of maps to describe what places are like; giving directions for routes.
Who killed Kit Marlowe?	● Use primary sources to form an opinion about an Elizabethan mystery.	Use sources in *The Reckoning* by Charles Nicholl (Jonathan Cape) to sequence the events of Marlowe's death and decide how he died.	● give reasons for their opinion about Marlowe's death	Write character sketches using details to evoke sympathy/dislike. Write a report on the murder.	
Who was William Shakespeare?	● Find out about the past from a range of sources and put them together. ● Understand that the past is represented in different ways.	Use various sources from the Internet to produce a Shakespeare timeline incorporating different elements.	● select and combine information for the timeline	Prepare read and perform playscripts. Chart the build-up of a play scene.	Drama: perform a selection of scenes from some of Shakespeare's plays.
Why did Drake circum-navigate the globe?	● Find out about the past from a range of sources. ● Understand that the past is represented in different ways.	Use accounts of Drake's voyage from the Internet and books to sequence the voyage and write a diary using selected information.	● select and combine information that demonstrates a particular view of the events	Collect information from a variety of sources and present it in a simple format.	Geography: use of the globe.
Why did England fight with Spain?	● Find out about the past from a range of sources. ● Understand that the past is represented in different ways.	Contrast the English and Spanish viewpoints (www.newadvent.org/cathen/01727c.htm). List reasons for the war in two columns.	● give both sets of reasons and understand the different viewpoints	Present points of view in writing. Use writing frames to illustrate points of view.	Citizenship: discuss how religious and political views divide people.
How was the Armada destroyed?	● Find out about the past from a range of sources and put them together. ● Understand that the past is represented in different ways.	Read extracts from the 'Fugger' letters on page 130 alongside secondary sources to understand why the accounts differ.	● answer questions about why the accounts differ	Write independently, linking own experiences to situations in historical stories.	
What do we know about Tudor times?	● Select and combine information to show change across a period.	Class activity: put aspects of era studied on a timeline. Children write their opinions about the most important features and changes.	● demonstrate an understanding of the main features of Tudor times and how things changed across the period.	Collect information from a variety of sources and present it in a simple format.	

CHAPTER 2

The
Elizabethan
age

1 hour What was Queen Elizabeth I like?

Learning objective
Use sources to answer questions that go beyond simple observations and draw deductions.

Lesson organisation
Whole-class introduction then individual work.

Vocabulary
portrait
ruff
farthingale
queen
monarch
Tudor

Background information

Tudor portraits, which provide the focus of this activity, are an essential source for children. The Tudor age was a time of individualism. In the Middle Ages pictures tended to depict the *idea* of kingship rather than the personal features of a particular monarch and we have little information about personalities and their idiosyncrasies. With the Renaissance came a great belief in human potential, and the potential of individuals.

There are a lot of portraits of Elizabeth which are easily available (a list of Internet sites is given below); they all show a recognisable person, but they are often also designed to send a message. Elizabeth used portraits as political tools. Some show Elizabeth, the woman, playing the part of Gloriana and Belphoebe – the virgin queen and sun of her people. The Armada portrait or the Rainbow portrait are excellent examples of this. The early portrait of Elizabeth as a girl in a red dress contrasts with these, but even there you will find clues about her preferred image. The open volume on a lectern and the prayer book in her hand show her as studious and religious, but there is also flamboyance and the desire to attract in her dress and demeanour.

What you need and preparation

Gather together a selection of portraits of Elizabeth – the National Portrait Gallery has postcard-sized reproductions, or download images from the Internet. These can be found at: www.royal.gov.uk/history/e1r.htm – the portrait of young princess Elizabeth at about 14; http://library.thinkquest.org/ 11775/monarchs/pictures/ElizabethI.jpg – this is the queen at about 30 before the Gloriana cult – it is still fairly natural; www.bangor.ac.uk/–hip01c/portrait.htm – three portraits and links to other sites; www.english.uiuc.edu/klein/420/ image_gallery.html – timeline of portraits. Make sure that you have enough images for one between two or three children. Prepare one picture as an OHT if possible or find an image in a book large enough to show to the whole class.

A Teacher's Guide to Using Portraits by Sue Wilkinson (English Heritage) has many more ideas you can use. You will also need: a portrait analysis sheet for each child (see 'Development'); board or flip chart; writing materials.

What to do

ICT opportunities
Create a *Hyperstudio* stack by downloading the portraits. Put invisible buttons over areas of the portraits that contain clues and connect them to cards with information about those clues.

15 mins Introduction

Ask the children to sit together on the carpet and explain that they are going to look at a portrait of someone from Tudor times and use it to find out about the person (you do not have to tell them that it is Tudor if you want them to talk first about the fact that the portrait is from a long time ago). Show the children the image and encourage them to look for clues about the person. Ask first what *sorts* of clues they could look for. These might be her clothes, what she is holding, what is in the background, what her face and hair are like. Investigate each aspect thoroughly, for example:

● What do her clothes tell us? (She was rich.)
● How can you tell? (She has lots of jewellery.)

Then go on to make a list of her jewellery, and move on to the next aspect. You can introduce vocabulary like *ruff* and *farthingale* (the hoop worn under a skirt to make it stand out). Talk about

the materials – real gold and silver thread were often used; silks came from China on camels and horses and took years to arrive.

In the later pictures, Elizabeth's face is very white because of the white lead powder she used and she wore a wig. Talk about how old she is. Ask about her expression (she usually looks serious but serene). Look at her hands – she was very proud of her long fingers and she made sure they were in the picture. Look for symbols around her; the book mentioned previously explains some of these.

List on the board the things that you have found out. Probably the fact that she was queen will come out early and you can tell the children her name.

30 mins Development

Divide the children into groups and allocate a different portrait of Elizabeth to each group, together with a framework sheet which they should complete as they analyse their picture. This should provide them with starter sentences and questions (see right).

Explain that they should analyse the clues first, then make hypotheses using the clues as evidence. It is fine to start with *I think she is a queen because she is wearing a crown* but encourage them to go on to *I think she is sad because she does not smile* or *I think she has been in a war because there are ships fighting in the background.* Circulate among the children and look out for comments which you can bring out in the plenary.

> **The portrait of Elizabeth I**
>
> Look at the portrait
> The person is wearing…
>
> The other things in the picture are…
>
> What sort of a person do you think this is?
>
> Why do you think that?

15 mins Plenary

Gather together the pictures of Elizabeth and form them into a timeline, starting with a picture of Elizabeth when she was young. Encourage the children to help you to sort them into chronological order.

Read out some of the children's observations and deductions that they made in the development work. Finish by showing that Elizabeth was queen for 43 years and went from being a shy, studious girl to a very powerful and astute woman.

Differentiation

Encourage less able children to use their observational skills to draw different elements of the portrait rather than writing about them. Invite them to contribute to the plenary.

Assessing learning outcomes

Can the children use the portraits to answer questions that go beyond simple observations and draw deductions?

> **Follow-up activity**
> Continue the portrait work, focusing on other Tudor personalities, such as Francis Drake and Sir Walter Ralegh, or contrast Elizabeth with Mary Queen of Scots. The children could compile a list of Elizabethan clothes as they analyse the pictures.

 How did Queen Elizabeth meet her people?

Background information

Elizabeth cared about personal popularity with ordinary people in a way that previous monarchs did not. The Spanish ambassador commented in 1568 that she was greeted by great acclamation everywhere she went, and he saw this as a peculiarly English phenomenon. The portraits built up an image of her in court circles, but the people needed to see her in person. In the summer the entire court usually mounted up and rode off on a royal progress into the more accessible parts of the kingdom. The tableware and tapestries and furniture were packed into 200-odd wagons and taken along. The queen could expect hospitality on request; the entire circus would descend on an

> **Learning objectives**
> ● Learn about how Elizabeth went on a royal progress.
> ● Demonstrate knowledge of some aspects of Elizabethan life.

Vocabulary
royal progress
curtsied
court usher
gentleman usher
yeoman purveyor
plague
manor
tapestry
palfrey
moppet
wardrobe officer
halberds
poleaxes

area, but all the evidence is that her visits were seen as a huge honour. Great lords would compete to put on lavish entertainment, but more humble houses were often chosen and the queen frowned on unnecessary expense and ostentation. She had a great way of giving time and kind words to the common people in the crowd and a graceful way of accepting simple tributes (like a branch of rosemary handed to her on her way to be crowned). She swore, and even threw things sometimes, at her ministers, but her graciousness in public became a legend that gave her unprecedented popularity.

The court included large numbers of aristocratic retainers like her ladies-in-waiting (who looked after her in her private rooms) and handsome young gentlemen serving as her official bodyguard. Her ministers such as William Cecil and Francis Walsingham and all their secretaries would need to be near her at all times as the government travelled with her. An army of servants was needed to cook and serve and empty latrines, to look after the hundreds of horses and set up beds and unpack linen. Lastly, anyone who claimed to be fashionable or had ambitions had to come along with their retainers.

What you need and preparation
Find some pictures of Elizabethan scenes, clothes, houses and so on in reference books. Cotehele House in Cornwall is a fine example of a Tudor manor like the one in the story (see photocopiable pages 122–3) and there is a picture of it at www.cata.co.uk/cotehele/images/cot.jpg. You may wish to create a writing frame for some children, as appropriate (see 'Differentiation'). You will also need: photocopiable pages 122–3; writing materials.

What to do
15 mins **Introduction**
Remind the children of the things they learned about Queen Elizabeth in the last activity and use the background information above to tell them a bit about a royal progress. Tell them that the story that you are going to read is fictional but is based on a real visit she made. Read 'The royal visit' on photocopiable pages 122–3 to the children, allowing them to follow the text on their own copies. Bring out the detail of the story by asking questions such as:
● Why did the usher come to check if anyone had had the plague (explain that this was a very infectious disease), before he approved the house?
● Why did Bet's father need to borrow money?
● Why did people go to so much trouble for such a short visit?
● What did the manor house look like? (Show some pictures of Tudor or pre-Tudor houses; also diamond-paned windows, panelling and tapestries.)
● What do you think a moppet was? (A doll.)
Go through the stages of the setting up of the visit, in the order that they are given in the story. Then talk about what the children think could have happened next:
● What do you think Queen Elizabeth would have done if a doll had dropped in her lap?
● What would Bet have done?
● What would Bet's father have thought and done?

30 mins **Development**
Explain that the children must imagine that they were there and write an account of the queen's visit. They can either continue the story, saying what happened next, or tell the story of the visit from a different point of view, such as Bet's father, the queen herself or a bystander.

Provide the children with pictures of Elizabethan scenes, clothes and houses and emphasise the importance of using the evidence to provide period details in the story.

 Plenary
Gather the children together and read out some accounts or parts of accounts that bring out good period detail and use the evidence.

Differentiation
Let less able children use a writing frame which follows the basic lines of the story and allows them to add detail. For example:
The first thing that Bet saw from the gatehouse was…
The next thing that happened was…
After Bet dropped the doll I think…

Assessing learning outcomes
Can the children write an account that incorporates period detail and is consistent with the evidence provided?

Follow-up activities
• Role-play the story on photocopiable pages 122–3, as a class, incorporating an ending that has been written by one of the children.
• Invite the children to draw the characters in the story and the house, Benhope Manor, where Queen Elizabeth stayed, and display them in the classroom.

What was the Elizabethan countryside like?

Background information
Most areas of Britain were rural in Tudor times. It is the earliest period for which there are comparatively good documentary records; this means that it should be possible for you to find local material to use for this topic. County or regional record offices will often have maps (you should be able to get a photocopy of part of a county, or larger-scale local map, from the period), manorial or parish records (there should be an education officer or educational adviser at the County Record Office or local history library who can advise you on these – such documents record things like the ownership of land, deaths from the plague, prosecutions for stealing pigs and so on). These sources will help the children to picture their local area in Tudor times and they will give real names of the people who lived there. They can be difficult to read in the original but children often enjoy decoding, with a key to help them, and translations can be provided.

Thomas Tusser wrote his *100 Good points of Husbandry* in 1557 and enlarged it to 500 good points in 1573. The idea behind it was to use the printing press and increased literacy to spread

ideas of good farming practice. There are a number of verses for each month, and children can enjoy learning some of the lines – they tell us a lot about the farming year in Tudor times. The entire work with commentaries that explain the meaning is published on the Internet at www.cla.org.uk/history/.

What you need and preparation
Prepare an enlarged copy of one of the verses from Tusser (see photocopiable page 124). You will also need: A4 copies of photocopiable page 124; a map of the local area in Elizabethan times (optional); pictures in reference books of the countryside in Elizabethan times, with illustrations of poor people's clothing and, if possible, farm tools; writing materials.

Learning objective
Use primary and secondary sources to gather information about aspects of life in the Elizabethan countryside.

Lesson organisation
Whole-class introduction, then individual or paired work

Vocabulary
See the glossary on photocopiable page 124.

What to do

Introduction

15 mins Tell the children that the area in which they live was countryside in Elizabethan times (presuming this is the case). If you have found a map of your local area that illustrates this, then show it to the class.

Ask them how most people earned their living in the country, and begin to talk about farming. Explain that the main crops were wheat for bread and barley for beer. Beans and greens would be grown, but potatoes were only brought back from America at the very end of Tudor times. Sheep were important because most clothes were woollen, and cattle were needed for milk, cheese and meat. Explore how much the children understand about the seasonal nature of agriculture – that most seeds are planted in early spring and that the harvest comes in late summer (children who live in urban areas may not know this). Tell them that Thomas Tusser wrote a long poem to help Elizabethan country people remember what to do in each month. Read a stanza together, for example:

> *January*
> Thy garden plot lately, wel trenched and mucked,
> would now be twifallowed, the mallowes plucked out:
> Wel clensed and purged, of root and of stone,
> that fault therein afterward, found may be none.

See how much of the text the children understand, and point out old-fashioned spellings such as *wel* and *clensed* and old words like *twifallowed* (the website above gives a full glossary). Enjoy saying the poem out loud together.

Development

30 mins Give individuals or pairs a stanza to work on from photocopiable page124. Talk about the month it comes from and discuss difficult words. Explain that their first task is to put the verse into modern English prose. For example, the one above might be:

> Your garden will now be well dug, with manure added;
> it will be dug twice and all the weeds pulled out –
> it must be cleaned of all roots and stones so that you
> cannot find anything wrong with it.

Then, using pictures provided for reference (encourage the children to find suitable pictures themselves from a selection of books), so that they can add realistic detail such as the clothes people are wearing, the children should illustrate the verse.

Plenary

15 mins Collect together the verses, translations and pictures and sequence them under the months. Go through them month by month and encourage the children to share what they have found out about the farming tasks to be done. In a number of cases the tasks are specific to men, women or children and you should point this out. Men tended to be involved in fieldwork like ploughing; women more with milking, processing and preserving meat, and gardening – both roles were essential.

ICT opportunities
Word-processing, research on the Internet and starting a Tudor dictionary database can all be incorporated into the activity.

Differentiation

For the development work, organise the children into mixed-ability pairs, so that more confident readers concentrate on deciphering the text, while less confident readers focus on drawing the pictures, finding suitable scenes and clothes in books and referring to them for accuracy.

Assessing learning outcomes

Can the children translate Tusser? Can they find and use appropriate pictures to source their illustrations?

Follow-up activities
● Use the text from Tusser in a presentation at an assembly, with miming of the tasks and reading of the verses.
● Let the children role-play a scene in a parish court; the parish court dealt with country matters like stealing pigs or moving fences. Your local history librarian may be able to provide you with an appropriate passage that you could use for information.

What was Elizabethan London like?

Background information

There were few cities of any size in Elizabethan England. Norwich, Bristol and Exeter were quite substantial and Plymouth grew steadily, but London stood alone, being about five times as big as any of the others. Not much remains of Elizabethan London. Westminster Abbey, Westminster Hall and the Tower are still there but the Great Fire cleared large areas of the timber-framed houses. London Bridge (the only bridge) was built with houses and shops, as the Ponte Vecchio in Florence still is.

The city was still surrounded by the Roman and Medieval walls, a short section of which can be seen near the Barbican. Within the walls, narrow streets with open drains running down the middle were overhung by projecting upper storeys; outside them were fields and market gardens that supplied the city's food. Streets were narrow and crowded and the greatest thoroughfare was the river, on which wherrymen were the taxi drivers of the day. Rich, powerful men had great houses along the river with their own landing stages. The city fathers, rich merchants, tended towards Puritanism and, increasingly, the seedy recreational district was established outside their jurisdiction across the Thames in Southwark.

Bull-baiting and bear-baiting, cruel sports that involved gambling, took place in wooden arenas rather like Roman ones. The red light district and taverns clustered around them. Later the Rose and the Globe theatres were built in a similar style alongside. Though the queen travelled in the summer, the court was based around London, in Whitehall, Greenwich, Nonesuch and the other palaces around the capital.

Learning objective
Use primary and secondary sources to gather information about aspects of life in Tudor London.

Lesson organisation
Whole-class introduction, then individual work.

Vocabulary
wherry
Westminster Abbey
bear-baiting
bull-baiting
timber-framed houses

What you need and preparation

Prepare the map on photocopiable page 125 as an OHT. You will also need: a modern map of London, large enough for all the children to see it clearly (the A–Z large street map of London is a good one, but any map that shows the river and the density of building will suffice); the video *Shakespeare in Love* (the scene in which Shakespeare takes a wherry to follow 'Master Kent', about 20 mins into the film (not essential but it brings the map to life with excellent period detail).

What to do

20 mins **Introduction**
Project the map on photocopiable page 125 onto the screen so that the children can all see it easily. Display the modern map nearby so they can see both. Ask the children to look for similarities and differences between Elizabethan and modern London.

● Similarities – the River Thames is not very different; London Bridge is in the same place; the Tower of London is much the same.

● Differences – Elizabethan London was much smaller; there are more fields; there were no railways and the roads are windier.

Encourage the children to tell you what they can say about Elizabethan London by looking at the map. Focus on:

● The River Thames; talk about the boats and their uses. On the Hogenburg map you can see wherries (taxis), big ships (all to the east of the bridge, which they could not get under, and towards the sea), smaller boats with sails carrying goods up and down the river (providing the same function as lorries today), long boats with many rowers (these were often private barges owned by rich men – the equivalent of limousines).

● Southwark. Show the bull-baiting and bear-baiting arenas and explain why they were there (see 'Background information').

● The walls. Show how abruptly the city ends and the country starts. Talk about the fact that there were no refrigerators, so produce had to be brought in every day, often by country girls with baskets. Show the market gardens where vegetables and fruit were grown and the cows, used for milk, butter and cheese.

If available, show the children a clip from *Shakespeare in Love*. Pause the video to point out the theatre (like the bear-baiting ring on the map, but not built when the map was drawn), river transport, the crowded streets and the characteristics of the houses.

30 **Development**
mins Ask the children to write about an imaginary walk across Elizabethan London, using the map on photocopiable page 125 for reference. They could imagine themselves as country people arriving from the north, passing the city gates, going through the noisy streets to the river. They should be able to trace their route on the map and they should describe the sights and sounds along the way.

15 **Plenary**
mins Read out some of the children's stories to the class, highlighting evocative and realistic detail that has been included.

ICT opportunities
The stories can be word-processed and displayed with the children's own drawings of Elizabethan London.

Differentiation

Allow the children to carry out the development work at three different levels. Ask more able children to write freely, making up a story which contains interesting incidents. Provide children of average ability with a writing frame: *When I came through the city gate I could see...* and so on. Invite less able children to draw a scene which depicts Elizabethan London and add captions.

Assessing learning outcomes

Can the children incorporate accurate information derived from the map (and the film) into their stories?

> **Follow-up activity**
> You may well be able to find other Tudor maps of your local area (in the local history library) which can be used to explore what has changed and remained the same.

① hour Who was William Shakespeare?

Background information

Shakespeare's reputation is unique amongst writers in English. He is probably the most famous writer in the world. As such, he is one figure that children ought to know something about. There is a huge amount of material on him, his work and his life so he makes an ideal research project.

What you need and preparation

Prepare research materials for several groups:

● Timeline group – prepare three or four accounts of Shakespeare's life. Some can be from children's books but others should be quite challenging. Internet accounts can be found at www.britguides.co.uk/shake.htm, www.stratford-upon-avon.co.uk/wslife.htm (long biography with good pictures), www.stratford.co.uk/hislife/hislife.html. There are also some facts about Shakespeare's life provided on photocopiable page 126. You will also need: A5 cards to peg on the timeline that is produced; a washing line and pegs.

● Picture group – prepare several pictures of Shakespeare (some are on www1.mwc.edu/–wkemp/gallery/shakespeare_images/shakimages1.htm) including the ones on photocopiable page 127. You will also need: a portrait analysis sheet for each child (see page 55); writing materials.

● Theatre group – find information and pictures of the Globe and other theatres. An image of the Globe is provided on photocopiable page 128, and you may find the following websites useful: www.rdg.ac.uk/globe/oldglobe/PrintsLondon.htm (images of the globe); www.rdg.ac.uk/globe/oldglobe/DeWitt.htm (picture of interior of the Swan theatre); http://shakespeares-globe.org/education/images/Elizabethans_at_Play.jpg (information on the education pack produced by the Globe theatre); http://shakespeares-globe.org/virtual-pictures/(a virtual Globe theatre). You can use the video of the film *Shakespeare in Love* to give the children impressions of the Rose theatre.

> **Learning objectives**
> ● Find out about the past from a range of sources and put them together.
> ● Understand that the past is represented in different ways.

> **Lesson organisation**
> Whole-class introduction, then group work.

What to do

ⓕ 15 mins Introduction

If you used *Shakespeare in Love* in the previous activity, then remind the children about it and perhaps show another short clip. Go on to give a brief introductory talk about Shakespeare, using some of the information from the sources above. Tell the children that they are going to find out more in groups, working individually or in pairs.

CHAPTER 2

The Elizabethan age

Vocabulary
whittawer
hornbook
poaching
plague
theatre company

ICT opportunities
Many of the Internet sources can be directly accessed and downloaded by the children, and captions and so on can be word-processed. A Shakespeare datafile could be produced or a *Hyperstudio* stack.

Follow-up activities
• Arrange a visit to the Globe theatre.
• To help children to appreciate the richness of Shakespeare's language, let them visit the Shakespearean insult kit website on www.crinos.com/users/aforte/features/shakespear/shakespear.insult.html.

Development

30 mins Provide each group with a set of research materials on their table, and explain how the children should carry out their tasks:

● The timeline group should read the accounts of Shakespeare's life and decide on five key points to write on separate 'timeline' cards. These may have dates on them or not. Make the choice simpler, if necessary, by preparing cards with questions on them, such as: *Shakespeare was born in… He married…* When the individuals or pairs have finished writing their cards they must discuss a logical order of the events and peg the cards onto a washing line (which you have previously hung up in the classroom) in the correct order.

● Ask the picture group to work on images of Shakespeare using the portrait analysis sheet. When they have finished they can timeline the pictures according to how old Shakespeare looks or when the picture was made (if they have this information). Ask them to discuss why there are differences between the pictures. Finally they can make a display of the pictures, with agreed captions.

● The theatre group can work on images of the Globe theatre and any other theatres from the Elizabethan period that you have obtained. They should talk about what they have learned from the picture and write captions. You can prepare questions if you wish: *Describe the shape of the theatre. Why do you think it was like this?* Finally they can make a display of the pictures, with agreed captions.

Plenary

15 mins Inivite the groups to present their work to the rest of the class. You should emphasise in each case the fact that different pictures and accounts represent the past in different ways.

Differentiation

The activities can be approached at different levels and less able children can use prepared questions as above.

Assessing learning outcomes

Can the children find out about the past from a range of sources and put them together? Can they understand that the past is represented in different ways?

① How was the Armada destroyed?
1 hour

Learning objectives
• Find out about the past from a range of sources and put them together.
• Understand that the past is represented in different ways.

Background information

The Armada is a big topic on which there is much information and it deserves to be treated over two or more lessons. General background information can be found at: www.britannica.com/bcom/eb/article/0/0,5716,9610+1,00.html; www.nmm.ac.uk/education/fact_armada.html; www.starnet.demon.co.uk/hawkins/hist.html; http://tbls.hypermart.net/history/1588armada (includes a database of ships involved and a firsthand account from a Spanish survivor of his landing in Ireland). A pro-Spanish point of view of the events can be found at: www.newadvent.org/cathen/01727c.htm. Queen Elizabeth's famous Tilbury speech is at: www.historyplace.com/speeches/elizabeth.html.

The Fuggers were fabulously rich German bankers and businessmen. Philip Fugger protected his business interests by employing correspondents to send news from all over Europe. His private news agency was probably the best of the time. Happily the letters were kept and an English translation was published in 1926.

The sailing of the Armada was big news and crucial to the Roman Catholic Fugger who might profit from a Spanish victory. The letters on photocopiable page 130 are simplified versions of a few of those relating to the Armada.

Traditionally, Sir Francis Drake has been given much credit for the defeat of the Armada. He certainly did much to provoke the invasion by his constant attacks on Spanish ships. He also delayed the Armada by his bold raids on Spanish ports where preparations were taking place. He did not command the English fleet (Lord Howard of Effingham was Admiral), but he was a very popular hero of the sea battles. The famous story of his refusal to abandon his game of bowls when the Armada was sighted may not be true, but it shows his public image as a cool customer. He attracted criticism from his superiors by seeming to prioritise the capture of valuable Spanish ships over obeying orders.

Elizabethan England saw the defeat of the Armada as a 'David and Goliath' victory by the underdog, and we still tend to do the same. Actually, the odds were not so uneven when you take into account the long lines of communication that handicapped the Spanish and, crucially, their terrible luck with the weather.

Lesson organisation
Whole-class introduction, then individual work.

Vocabulary
Armada
galleons
merchant

What you need and preparation
Make a large copy for display, or a copy for each group, of photocopiable page 129. Produce an OHT of the facsimile newspaper at: http://www.exmsft.com/-davidco/History – this would be useful but it is not essential. You will also need: photocopiable page 130 (cut up to produce simpler differentiated sections, if necessary); atlases for the children with a map of Europe showing the places mentioned on photocopiable page 129; a large simple map of Europe (showing Hamburg, Middleburg, Prague, Cadiz, Plymouth, Calais and Gravelines); writing materials.

What to do
15 mins **Introduction**
Outline the reasons for the Spanish wanting to invade England (see photocopiable page 129):
● Because Philip thought he had a right to be king of England, as he had been Queen Mary's husband
● Because the Roman Catholics in England wanted Philip to be king
● Because English pirates like Francis Drake kept attacking Philip's treasure ships and stealing his treasure.

Tell the children how the Armada set sail on 21 July, and look at the timeline of events together to familiarise them with what happened.

Explain how, without radios and telephones, it was hard to get news of what was happening in other places. Talk about Philip Fugger and how he got people to write letters to him about what was going on. Say how those letters had to come by ship and horseback and they took a long time to get to their destination. Because news was hard to get, false rumours and information often got about. The heading of the facsimile newspaper shows this (see website address above).

30 mins **Development**
Give the children one or more of the Fugger letters on photocopiable page 130. Write some key questions on the board (see overleaf), run through them and ask the children to write individual or group answers.

**ICT
opportunities**
● There is plenty of
information on the
Internet that
children can access
(also see website
address on page
63).
● Follow-up stories
can be word-
processed.

**Follow-up
activities**
Children can write
an imaginary
account linked to
one of the letters.
They might be a
sailor with
Limburger, for
instance.
Encourage them to
use other evidence,
such as pictures, in
order to add colour
to their descriptions
of the ships and
people.

● What are the main points of information given in the account?
● Do you think the account is accurate?
● If it is accurate, find out from the timeline when the events described actually happened.
● Look at the atlas to find the place where the letter was written. How long did the news take to get there?

 Plenary

Using a map of Europe and the timeline, go through some of the children's responses, emphasising that we, looking back, are in a better position to have all the facts; the accuracy of the accounts depends on where the information came from (Hans Limburger's information was firsthand and accurate, whereas quite false stories were circulating in Prague long after the event).

If you have time, discuss other questions such as:
● Why were the English happy that the Armada was coming? (Perhaps because it ended the suspense of waiting, or perhaps they were very confident of winning.)
● Why did people in Prague celebrate when they thought the English were beaten? (Because they were Catholics and supported Spain.)

Differentiation

More able children should be able to deal with all the accounts and contrast them. Less able children could be given just one account to analyse. Where possible, a group of weaker readers might work with an adult helper on a group response.

Assessing learning outcomes

Can the children find out about the past from a range of sources and put them together? Can they understand that the past is represented in different ways?

World history

The world study units specified in the National Curriculum provide a choice between seven ancient civilisations that grew up in different parts of the world. In selecting a world study unit it may well be appropriate to think about how the unit can widen the children's historical perspective, for example by including vibrant and valid examples of black history. It is also important to review regularly which units are studied. Don't be afraid to try something completely different occasionally. The guidance provided on the breadth of study is minimal and this leaves schools with an ideal opportunity to develop a unit of study that is imaginative and innovative.

One of the drawbacks of the world study units has often been their lack of recognisable personalities or features. This makes it more difficult to identify key elements in these relatively unknown periods than it is for our own history. This lack of recognisable personalities has also meant that the story element that is so important in making history come alive is also lacking. To tackle this problem, both the units selected as exemplars in this chapter include substantial background information and reference sources to supplement your own research. Stories about fictional characters have been included to help bring the period to life and encourage children to think about those who might have lived in that far distant past.

We have chosen to develop two of the world study units. One of the units – Ancient Egypt – is well known, the other – Benin – is perhaps less familiar. Ancient Egypt is probably the most popular and well resourced of the world study units. There is a wealth of primary as well as secondary material at the level of both the child and the adult. The large number of websites dedicated to the period testify to the enduring fascination that Ancient Egypt produces.

Benin is an exciting and colourful unit to choose. As a civilisation that flourished around the same time as the Tudors in this country it offers an additional element to develop the children's understanding of the period. It allows children to compare and contrast the lifestyles of two societies that grew up in different parts of the world around the same time. It also provides a positive model of a black civilisation that interacted on an equal basis with Europeans.

Ancient Egypt

Ancient Egypt is, without doubt, the most popular of the world study units and the one that you are most likely to see in school. What is it about this topic that is so alluring to children at Key Stage 2? It is visually very exciting, with vast sculptures and structures covered in strange and exotic images. It is full of fascinating, and yet somehow repelling, practices such as the preparation of mummies. It is also coloured by the impressions given to us by the treasures of Tutankhamun's tomb – that of wealth and privilege and everywhere 'the glint of gold'. While it is true that the pharaohs were fabulously wealthy, there is more to this period and civilisation than bizarre alien artefacts and icons. It is import that children understand the reasons why the Egyptian civilisation developed at that time and in that place and why it was so influential for so long.

The Ancient Egyptian civilisation extended over a very long period and it is sometimes difficult for children to comprehend this wide sweep of time. There were many modifications during this period as the civilisation developed and changed. Life for an early Egyptian bore little resemblance to that of someone living at the time of Cleopatra. While the use of timelines will allow children to develop their understanding of the chronology of the time, it is impossible to investigate all of the period in equal depth. It is necessary therefore to be selective in order to identify relevant areas of

investigation. It is important to centre these areas of investigation on an important individual of whom there is a variety of information to be discovered. This would obviously point to a prominent pharaoh. There are a number of interesting individuals from different eras within the period. Some of the people that would reward investigation are Hatshepsut and Tuthmosis III, Rameses II, or Cleopatra. 'Life in Egyptian times' can then be related to life at that particular point in Egyptian history rather than trying to cover the whole period.

Akhenaten and Tutankhamun have been chosen as examples for this unit because they lived at a time of conflict and change, when the pharaoh, and through him Egypt, were reassessing traditional beliefs and the way of life. There is a mystery about how the two pharaohs died, whether their deaths were from natural causes or murder. These ancient mysteries can stimulate children's interest in discovering more about the people and in trying to find an answer to the questions. Through the discovery of Tutankhamun's tomb and the excavations at Tell el Amarna there is a wealth of archaeological evidence about the period and strong links to our own time. By centring on a particular individual, it is possible to strengthen the human element of the study and to give the period a human face.

The children should also understand the importance of the River Nile to the development of life in Egypt. The River Nile provided the lifeblood for the civilisation's development. It provided water to irrigate the desert land and allowed the cultivation of crops that supported the growing population. The seasonal floods regularly deposited fertile black mud along the length of the river. The Egyptians were therefore able to rely on the continual renewal of their land. During the period of the inundation people were unable to work on the land as normal and so the pharaohs were able to mobilise this workforce for their major building projects such as pyramid or temple construction. The Nile also provided an important communication and transport link. The prevailing winds blew in one direction while the currents of the river flowed in the opposite direction. This facilitated travel up and down the river. Goods could be delivered from north to south and vice versa. People were also mobile, which meant that information and ideas could be spread throughout the Empire.

One of the fundamental contradictions of this complex civilisation is that while Egypt was a fertile and fecund land surrounded by growth, the major preoccupation of the people was with death or more specifically life after death. Egyptians sought to ensure that their souls would be safe in the afterlife and so spent their whole lives preparing for death. They worked hard to gather enough wealth so that after they died, they were properly equipped with possessions they might need in the afterlife. Their bodily remains were mummified and it was a duty of those left behind to ensure that all the complicated formulas and rituals were performed correctly. The mummification process is one that fascinates many children and this provides a strong incentive to investigate the period. However, it is important that children understand why the Egyptians practised mummification as well as how they did it. Building a copy of an Egyptian sarcophagus has little point if children do not know what it would have been used for or why it was important.

The study unit of the Ancient Egyptians will always fascinate and enthral children by its lavish and exotic characteristics. It is important to see past the gold and curious images to try to see faces of the people who lived at that time, both rich and poor. Children need to begin to understand why the civilisation developed and flourished at that time and in that place, and how the beliefs of the period influenced the lifestyles of those who lived then. They should also begin to understand the part that archaeology has played in developing our understanding of the far distant past.

UNIT: Ancient Egypt

Enquiry questions	Learning objectives	Teaching activities	Learning outcomes	Literacy links	Cross-curricular links
What did Howard Carter find?	● Use sources to stimulate and help answer questions about the past.	Use accounts of Carter's discovery of Tutankhamun's tomb to begin to understand the role of the archaeologist.	Children: ● explain why Carter's find was important ● begin to understand the work of archaeologists	As a group, write the front page of a newspaper reporting the discovery of the tomb.	Citizenship: discuss the morality of archaeological investigations: was Carter desecrating a tomb by opening it?
What can we find out about the 'Boy King'?	● Find answers from sources that go beyond simple observation to make deductions.	Look at examples of Tutankhamun's possessions to decide what sort of person he was.	● make deductions about the lifestyle that Tutankhamun had from looking at his possessions	Make a catalogue of articles found in his tomb, giving descriptions and probable usage.	Science: investigate the type of materials used and how different materials decayed.
What was a pharaoh like?	● Demonstrate an understanding of main events and people.	Look through pictorial sources to find other examples of images of pharaohs.	● select the pharaohs from the different images	Give written justification for their answers.	
What happened after death?	● Select and combine information from sources.	Research the afterlife and the 'Book of the Dead'. Play the game on the back of the British Museum activity book.	● use a variety sources to find out what the Egyptians thought would happen after death	Write a diary of a journey after playing the game.	
How was Akhenaten different?	● Show how aspects of the past have been represented and interpreted in different ways.	Read the story of Nerfer-tari. Look at why Akenaten was not a typical pharaoh and why he created a cult of Aten.	● explain how Akhenaten was different and why he was unpopular with some of society	Look at some of Akhenaten's poetry. Use it to create your own poems in a similar style.	Art: contrast the painting from Amarna with the previous formal style used for royal portraits.
What were the pyramids for?	● Produce structured work making appropriate use of dates and times.	Discuss why the pharaohs built the pyramids and how they went about building them.	● explain why the pyramids were built and why certain methods were used	Write instructions for building a pyramid. Use labelled diagrams.	Maths/design and technology: examine construction of pyramids; build a scale model.
What made Egypt great?	● Give reasons for and results of main events and changes.	Look at the Nile's inundations and how they and other physical features of Egypt allowed the civilisation to grow.	● give reasons why the Nile was important to the development of the Egyptian civilisation	Use reference texts and CD-ROMs to research the effect of the Nile's annual inundations.	Geography: investigate the River Nile and its effect on the settlement of the region past and present.
How do we know about the Ancient Egyptians?	● Select and combine sources of information.	Look at the importance of the scribes. Look at how hieroglyphs were used. Investigate how archaeologists used the Rosetta Stone.		Use *Pepi and the Secret Names*, Jill Paton Walsh, to create a secret name for yourself. Write the name in hieroglyphs.	Art: repeat patterns and stylised art forms for tomb painting; large-scale paintings for class display.
How did the rich and the poor live?	● Identify changes within the period.	Use information from British Museum website to research the daily routine of a rich and a poor man.	● identify differences between the lives of rich and poor ● explain why there may be differences		
What did people believe in?	● Give reasons why people in the past acted as they did.	Individual research to investigate the belief system of the Egyptians. Look at the different cults of the gods and goddesses.	● explain why the gods were important to the Egyptians ● recognise importance of the role of scribes	Create a page for a class book on an Egyptian god or goddess. Describe the divinity and his or her roles.	RE: look at Ancient Egyptian religion and belief in the afterlife; contrast monotheistic and polytheistic beliefs in Ancient Egypt.
What was life like in the city?	● Demonstrate knowledge and understanding of characteristic features of past societies and periods.	Listen to the story of Imhotep and the water garden. Use paintings, accounts and plans to gain an impression of what the city was like.	● recognise different features of the city.	Write a paragraph describing a walk through the city.	Geography: mapping skills – use maps of the city and plans of buildings to help visualise what the place was like.

① What did Howard Carter find?

Learning objective
Use sources to stimulate and help answer questions about the past.

Lesson organisation
Whole-class introduction followed by group tasks; whole-class plenary.

Vocabulary
archaeologist
Egyptology
tomb
excavation
artefacts
antiquities
hieroglyphs
cartouche
seal
sponsor
patron

Background information

Modern Egyptology probably owes its origins to Napoleon's campaigns along the Nile in the 18th century, when Europeans first arrived in large numbers in the Nile Valley. It was at this time, in 1799, that the Rosetta Stone was discovered. This artefact, which had the same text written on it in three different languages, including Ancient Egyptian transcribed in hieroglyphs, allowed historians to decipher hieroglyphs and therefore begin to unravel the information recorded in thousands of inscriptions around the land. Throughout the 18th and 19th centuries there was an interest in seeing antiquities from the mysterious Nile. This led to wholesale looting of tombs by rich Europeans who carried their souvenirs home. Many wealthy enthusiasts sponsored 'excavations'. One of these was Lord Carnarvon. Due to bad health the peer had been ordered to winter in the dry climate of the Nile. Here he met and subsequently became the patron of Howard Carter. Carnarvon sponsored many years of relatively fruitless digging in the Valley of the Kings (one of the central burial sites for the ancient pharaohs). Finally, after ten long years of searching, Carter discovered a set of steps leading below ground. When he saw that the funeral seals were still intact, he sent for Carnarvon before beginning to open the tomb. Twenty-two days after finding the steps the door was cracked open. The flickering light of a candle threw shadows of fantastic shapes against the whitewashed walls and caught the enticing glint of gold. Carter, Carnarvon and their team had found the last tomb of the 'Boy King' Tutanhkamun.

Further information can be found on a variety of websites, but a good starting point is: www.ancientegypt.co.uk.

Useful reference books include:
The Search for Ancient Egypt by Jean Vercoutter (Thames & Hudson);
Pharaohs of Egypt by Jacquetta Hawkes (Cassell) – good for adult reference;
Millennium Eyewitness by Brian Stone (Piatkus);
History Detectives by Bruce Jameson (Oliver & Boyd).

What you need and preparation

Collect together a selection of reference books with photographs and a plan of the tomb. You will also need: individual copies of photocopiable pages 131 and 132; notepaper and clipboards. Set up the classroom as if for a news conference.

What to do

⑮ Introduction

Explain to the children that they are to imagine that they are newspaper reporters. They are going to attend a news conference such as they may have seen on television. You will be playing the part of someone who has something to tell the reporters. You will be describing something your character discovered. The reporters need to make notes so that they can write a newspaper account. Explain that they will have a list of questions and that they should listen carefully to your report to find the answers to the questions. Hand out clipboards, notepaper and photocopiable page 132.

Once the children are settled, leave the classroom. Re-enter in the role of Howard Carter, bringing with you the reference books with illustrations of the tomb. Hand out copies of photocopiable page 131. Take a central position, sit down and introduce your character. Relate the main points of the story while the children take notes using photocopiable page 132. Use the plan of the tomb and images of what was found to illustrate points.

After the 'press conference' allow time for questions. If the children do not ask questions and

there are areas that remain uncovered then feed in additional information. You will need to ensure that you have provided answers to all the questions on photocopiable page 132, for example you will need to tell them how long Carter worked in the Valley of the Kings.

35 mins Development
Split the children into groups. Ask each group to create a newspaper article reporting Carter's find using the press release on page 131 and the notes they have taken from the 'press conference'.

You may want to structure the task by giving the children specific elements that the article should have such as a headline, introduction, main text, picture and caption. You may also want to give them a mock-up of a page so that they know how much room they have.

10 mins Plenary
Ask one child from each group to explain how their group have organised their page and read their main headline.

Differentiation
Information sheets could be created to include either a simplified or more complex text. Adult support may be needed to help organise lower-ability groups.

To extend the activity for more able children, use *Ancient Lands* CD-ROM to watch archive footage of Howard Carter and his excavation (Map>Egypt>Monuments and Mysteries>Valley of the Kings>Howard Carter). The children should report back on any additional information they have discovered and answer the following questions: *What impression does the film give of the interest aroused by Carter's discovery? What do you think of the type of people who flocked to see the tomb and why do you think this?*

Assessing learning outcomes
Can the children explain what Carter found and why it was important? Can they explain why the story captured the attention of the public?

ICT opportunities
Use a desktop publishing package to set up and word-process reports using different fonts and sizes for different types of text. Scan in and position plans and illustrations.

Follow-up activity
Children will probably need additional time to refine, draft and copy out finished pieces onto their newspaper page.

---

1 hour What can we find out about the 'Boy King'?

Background information
Tutankhamun became pharaoh at a time of turmoil and division. The previous pharaoh, Akhenaten, had been a radical whose reforms had split the country. He had challenged the power of the priests by instigating a new religion and by moving his capital from Thebes to the centre of the country at Tell el Amarna. Here he built a stunning series of new palaces and named the new capital Akhetaten.

Tutankhaten, as Tutankhamun was known as a child, was related to the royal family of Akhenaten and his wife Nefertiti. He grew up surrounded by the beauty of the city of Akhetaten and later married Akhenaten's third daughter, Ankhesenpaaten, who was a few years older than himself. When Tutankhaten was nine years old, the pharaoh Akhenaten and his heir Smenkhkare died mysteriously and the young Tutankhaten was proclaimed pharaoh. As pharaoh, he moved the capital back to Thebes and changed his name to Tutankhamun to show his allegiance to the old gods, which the previous pharaoh, Akhenaten had rejected. Tutankhamun and Ankhesenamen, as his wife was now called, lived a life of ease and privilege, travelling the country living in one beautiful palace or another, surrounded by servants and slaves. Pictures of them show a tenderness between them which suggests that they were genuinely attached to one another. Tutankhamun only ruled for about nine years, however, and died aged eighteen or nineteen. His death may have

Learning objectives
● Find answers that go beyond simple observations to make deductions.
● Show an awareness that the past is divided into different periods of time.

Vocabulary
pharaoh
chariot
gold
lapis lazuli
precious jewels
faience
alabaster
chest
coffer
casket
furniture
lion headed
stool
throne
gilt
gilded
funeral barge
flail and crook
statue
ushabatis

been an accident or it may have been murder – Egypt was full of intrigue at this time and his skull shows evidence of a blow. It could be that the controlling priesthood – who had spent Tutankhamun's reign removing any evidence of the contamination of the old pharaoh's ideas – murdered Tutankhamun once he became older and they could no longer control him. Tutankhamun left no living heirs, although two mummified still-born infants were found alongside him in the tomb. After Tutankhamun's death, Ankhesenamen tried to marry a Hittite prince. However, the prince was murdered and Ankhesenamen later disappeared!

Little would have been known about the 'Boy King' Tutankhamun and his insignificant reign had his tomb not been the only one to survive almost untouched until the present day.

Further information can be found in a variety of reference books and websites:
www.argonet.co.uk/users/harts/egypt – information on all the main characters. It includes colour images of the tomb of Tutankhamun and descriptions of individual items found;
The Boy Pharaoh Tutankhamun, Noel Streatfeild (Michael Joseph) – this gives some good background to the story and has some excellent photos of the artefacts;
The Complete Tutankhamun, Nicholas Reeves (Thames & Hudson) – this has excellent photographs of artefacts, photos taken of the tomb as it was cleared and Howard Carter's sketches showing where everything was found.

What you need and preparation
Gather together reference books that show examples of the artefacts found within the tomb and pictures of the newly opened tomb. Make a timeline and draw a selection of images to represent different eras that the children have studied. You will also need: photocopiable pages 133 and 134 (enough for one of each per child); Blu-Tack.

What to do

 Introduction
Show the children the image of what the tomb looked like when it was first opened. Ask the children what impression it gives them of the importance of the tomb and its inhabitant. Does it look tidy? Do the objects look like the sorts of things the children have in their homes? Are there any objects that look unusual or exotic? Ask the children if they can tell, just by looking at the picture, what sort of person owned the objects. Carter thought that he had found a pharaoh's tomb. Ask the children if they think that the contents prove this. Do they think we can learn anything about the sort of life the person had from looking at his possessions?

30 mins **Development**
Give out copies of photocopiable pages 133 and 134 to the children and split them into groups so that resources can be shared. Ask the children to use reference books, CD-ROM or Internet facilities to find pictures of the objects found in the tomb. Tell them to select three objects each to investigate. Ask them to fill in the questions asked on their photocopiable pages. Circulate and support. Point out specific features to the children such as what the ushabatis were (models of servants and slaves to work for the dead person in the afterlife).

 Plenary
Bring the class back together to look at the timescale involved in the study of the period. Using the timeline created, start with the present and then locate the 1920s on the timeline to show when Carter found the tomb. Move back along the timeline, attaching the pictures to it with Blu-Tack to mark different periods, especially those which have been or will be studied in Key Stage 1 and Key Stage 2. Encourage the children to try to pinpoint different periods and add pictures themselves. Show them the Ancient Egyptian period on the timeline and begin to put in

any famous people they have already encountered. Point out that the period is a long one and so not everything can be covered. This study will concentrate on the period of Ahkenaten and Tutankhamun. Identify any specific people or events that will be investigated during the study. Children can add other pictures or information if they discover any.

Differentiation

Sort the reference books so that there are simple information books available for those who need them. Provide pictorial vocabulary sheets to help children identify different artefacts.

To extend the activity, ask more able children to research the lives of Tutankhamun and Ankhesenamen and tell their story to the rest of the class.

Assessing learning outcomes

Can the children make deductions about the type of lifestyle that Tutankhamun had from looking at his possessions? Can they locate the Ancient Egyptian era on the timeline?

How was Akhenaten different?

Background information

Amenhotep IV succeeded his father as pharaoh in about 1353BC. Over the 17 years that he ruled, he came to stamp his character on every aspect of Egyptian life. He was to become one of the best known of the Egyptian pharaohs, not least for his enigmatic connection to Tutankhamun which may have led to that young king's murder. By the end of his life he was known to his former subjects as 'the heretic pharaoh' or 'the criminal of Akhetaten'. What had he done to deserve such epitaphs? Amenhotep IV was not a warrior like his father. He was physically very unprepossessing, with a long face, stooped shoulders, thick thighs and a sagging stomach! He was not interested in foreign conquest but was a visionary and a dreamer who was passionate about religion. He came to believe that one god should take precedence over the rest of the established pantheon. The god he selected was not the powerful Amun-Re but Aten, a sun god depicted by a golden disc sending forth rays of light that nurtured all life. This change of allegiance from the long-established religious tradition of worshipping many gods to a monotheistic belief brought him into direct conflict with the power of the priests, which eventually led to his downfall.

Amenhotep changed his name to Akhenaten to show his new-found devotion. He moved his capital from Thebes, and the priests, to a site known as Akhetaten, 'The Horizon of Aten', where there was a small village called Tell el Amarna. Here, Akhenaten built a new city and lived there with his beautiful and charismatic queen Nefertiti and their six daughters. He filled the city with artists and craftsmen who were encouraged to move away from the stylised representation of life to one which was much more realistic. One of the best examples of this style, which became known as the Amarna style, is the famous bust of Nefertiti. Akhenaten himself composed the *Great Hymn to Aten* – one of the earliest examples of Egyptian poetry. After Akhenaten's death, the balance of power swung back to the priests and they attempted to erase all evidence of the pharaoh and his heresy.

There are a number of websites that give further in-depth information. Look for key words of Akhenaten, Amarna,

Learning objective
Show how aspects of the past have been represented and interpreted in different ways.

Lesson organisation
Whole-class story, followed by group investigative tasks; whole-class plenary.

Vocabulary
realism
artist
sculptor
priest
temple
stylised form
Aten

Akhetaten, Nefertiti and Aten. Some useful sites include:

www.argonet.co.uk/users/harts/egypt/3a_amen.htm – for Akhenaten;

www.argonet.co.uk/users/harts/egypt/8_gods.htm#godaten – for Aten.

What you need and preparation

Collect reference books with pictures and information about Akhenaten and Nefertiti. Print out information from some of the websites about Akhenaten. Organise Internet facilities so that children can research the topic on the Internet. You will also need: photocopiable pages 135–8; poster-sized paper; writing and drawing materials.

What to do

(20 mins) Introduction

Read the story on photocopiable pages 135 and 136 to the children. Discuss the aspects of Egyptian life covered in the story. Bring out the following points:

● Akhenaten was very much a family man and included his family in his public life. Women seemed to have had a high status at Akhetaten as was shown by the prominence of Nefertiti. The little princesses were also seen as important even though they could not directly inherit the throne.

● Akhenaten changed the way that people worshipped the gods, moving from a polytheistic to monotheistic religion. This was not universally popular.

● Akhenaten encouraged artists and craftsmen to live in his new city of Akhetaten. He also encouraged artists to experiment with new ways of portraying both the natural world and individuals. This artistic style was much more realistic than the traditional style had been.

(30 mins) Development

Split the class into groups. Give each group either photocopiable page 137 or 138. Explain to the children that each group will research either aspects of Akhenaten's life or the worship of Aten. Tell each group to use the pages to structure their research and to help them make a poster about their subject.

Ask each group to select two interesting facts that they have found out to share with the rest of the class in the plenary session. Also ask each group to nominate a spokesperson.

(20 mins) Plenary

Ask the spokesperson from each group to show the poster that they have produced and to tell the rest of the class the two interesting facts they have selected.

Add Akhenaten and Nefertiti to the class timeline if they have not already been added.

Take ideas from the children about why they think that Akhenaten was not a typical pharaoh. These could be added to the display with the posters.

Differentiation

The questions for group 1 on page 137 are aimed at less able groups as there is more comprehension and less inference required. Adult support may be necessary to organise information gathering within the group and to assign tasks.

The questions for group 2 on page 138 are aimed at more able groups as they encourage children to make deductions and draw inferences from the information. They also require more effective research skills as the information is less obvious.

Assessing learning outcomes

Can the children explain how Akhenaten was different and why he was unpopular with some elements of society?

(1 hour) What were the pyramids for?

Background information

Although the best-known pyramids are found at Giza there are the remains of about 80 pyramids scattered across Egypt. The pyramids were conceived as gigantic and elaborate tombs to house the bodies of pharaohs. This particular form of royal tomb grew out of earlier, more conventional mausoleums. The mastaba tomb was a large, rectangular, flat-topped building with graduated or sloped sides. The building was usually made of mud bricks with burial chambers and underground rooms cut into the bedrock. The earliest recognisable pyramid was the step pyramid of King Djoser at Saqqara. It was built by Imhotep around 2650BC and is the oldest large stone building in the world. This pyramid rises 60 metres in a series of six progressively diminishing terraces. It was the major feature in a complex of funerary architecture, including mortuary chapels. It is the complex at Giza that is most well known, however, and this is the only one of the Seven Wonders of the Ancient World that has survived to the present. The site at Giza contains three pyramids – the Great Pyramid of Khufu (built around 2589–2566BC), and those of his son Khafra and his grandson Menkaura – as well as the enigmatic Sphinx. Extensive excavations of the site have helped archaeologists come to a better understanding of how these massive structures were constructed. It is believed that about 20 000 to 30 000 men and women were involved in building each pyramid. Many of these workers would have been local farmers who took part in the construction during the periods of the Nile's annual inundation. The flooding of the river also allowed huge blocks of stone to be floated down the Nile to the site. The building of the pyramids were gigantic feats of engineering that involved precise calculations and careful surveys. Although unsophisticated, the technology was enormously effective. It was a technology that was used to serve the needs of the dead rather than the living.

Further information can be found in most books and websites on Ancient Egypt, including:
www.pbs.org/wgbh/nova/pyramid – this is an excellent site with images, diagrams, virtual reality tours and information on the site at Giza. It also includes fascinating interviews with archaeologists working on the site;
An Introduction to Egyptology by James Putnam (Grange Books) – this has a chapter with background information at adult level;
Egyptian Pyramid (Watch it grow) by Elizabeth Longley (Macdonald Young Books);
Awesome Egyptians by Terry Deary (Scholastic);
Ancient Eygpt by Dr George Hart (Macdonald Young Books).

Learning objectives
● Produce structured work, making appropriate use of dates and terms.
● Give reasons for and results of the main events of a period.

Lesson organisation
Whole-class discussion and investigation followed by individual research.

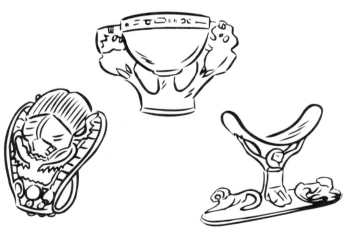

What you need and preparation

Collect together a large, heavy weight, such as a box of books, at least three rollers such as lengths of dowelling and something to act as a lever. Set up the weight at the front of the room and organise the class so that all children will be able to see the demonstration. Mark out a point A on the floor and another, B, a little further on. At point A, use the lever to raise the front of the weight onto one of the rollers.Roll the weight along and add another roller under the front of the weight. Keep rolling the weight along, replacing rollers at the front of the weight when they leave the weight at the back until you reach point B.

Ancient Egypt

Vocabulary
pyramid
engineering
technology
quarry
limestone
granite
survey
measurement
angle
builders
stonemasons
ramps
design
sledge
construction
block
sphinx
lever
roller

Practise using the equipment as described to move the weight from A to B so that you are clear how it works. Leave the weight at point A in full view of the class, but ensure that the rollers and levers are out of sight initially.

Find reference books and other information about the pyramids. Collect together images of pyramids including one which shows the scale of the Great Pyramid at Giza. Display the images of the pyramids to the best advantage, so that they create dramatic impact. You will also need: photocopiable pages 139–140; paper; writing materials.

What to do

20 mins **Introduction**

Tell the children that you have a problem and need their help to try to find a solution. Show them the weight and explain that you want to move it. Choose one of the children to be Seneb – an Egyptian foreman working at the site of the pyramids – and some other children to be his 'gang of workers'. Seneb needs to arrange to have the weight moved from point A to point B. Encourage the children to make suggestions that might help Seneb, for example pushing, pulling, lifting, getting the school caretaker to help, finding a little trolley with wheels. Explain that Seneb didn't have any wheeled trolleys or carts to help him and that there were no machines. Allow children to try out some of their suggestions but stress health and safety issues and do not allow children to strain themselves.

If the children do not suggest rollers, a lever or sledge, show the children the equipment. Ask them to guess how it might be used and what would be the drawbacks of using something like this. Again allow time for practical demonstration with Seneb and his 'gang of workers'. Bring out the following points in the discussion:

● The method is effective but very labour intensive.
● The method is slow and so the project would not be completed in a hurry.
● The method requires a lot of physical strength and effort. Workers would need to be strong and fit.

Tell the children to look at pictures of the pyramids, especially ones that show the scale of the structures. What do the children think about how they were made? What problems do they think the ancient builders had to overcome? What do they think the pyramids were used for?

Explain that they will be doing some research to try to find the answers to these and other questions. They will be trying to find out how and why the pyramids were built.

40 mins **Development**

Settle the children at tables with a collection of reference material. Give each group a copy of photocopiable page 139 or 140. Explain that they must use the reference material to find the answers to the questions, and then use their answers as a basis for writing a structured account of why and how the pyramids were built. Give the children 20 minutes to research their answers and then 20 minutes to turn their answers into a report.

After the children have collected answers to the questions, ask them to put them together using dates and specific terms related to the period and the activities taking place. Explain that they need to write a report using the title from their differentiated set of questions. The children can also include information gained from the demonstration.

Differentiation

The different groups of questions are graduated in terms of the demands they make on children. The first set of questions on page 139 tends to encourage mainly reading comprehension. There is more deduction and inference expected within the second group of questions on page 139. The questions on page 140 expect children to use textbooks as a basis for drawing their own conclusions.

Adult support may be needed to help lower-ability children use the textbooks.

Assessing learning outcomes

Can the children explain why the pyramids were built and why certain construction methods were used?

(1 hour) How do we know about the Ancient Egyptians?

Background information

Ancient Egyptian is one of the oldest recorded languages. It was used from approximately 3100BC to AD394 and is still in use in some form in Coptic religious services. The Ancient Egyptians had a number of writing systems for transcribing their language, including the pictorial hieroglyphs. Hieroglyphic script was endowed with religious and magical properties and was usually associated with stone inscriptions. A hieroglyphic inscription was traditionally arranged in columns. For most administrative and business affairs as well as for literary and mathematical texts, another script, called Hieratic, was used. Hieratic script was written with a brush and ink on papyrus or pottery. Although it took 12 years to train as a scribe, many Egyptian boys chose to take the training because of the great power scribes held. They controlled the ability to record deeds for posterity and were well paid.

The hieroglyphic system was confusing for archaeologists to decipher because it does not work in the same way as our alphabet does. Some hieroglyphs give pictorial indications of whole words (ideograms) and some represent sounds, either individually or in groups (phonograms). There is no punctuation to mark the end of sentences or the spaces between words. Text can be read from right to left, left to right or up and down. A bird's beak points to the beginning of the sentence. The hieroglyphic system was finally cracked by Jean-Francois Champollian after he discovered the Rosetta Stone in 1799. The Rosetta Stone (which can be seen in the British Museum) has the same text inscribed on it three times: in two different Ancient Egyptian scripts, and in Ancient Greek. Using his knowledge of Ancient Greek, Champollian was able to decode the hieroglyphs. The pharaohs' names provided the key to working out the rest of the letters.

Further information can be found in:

Find Out About Ancient Egypt by Philip Steele (Southwater);

Ancient Egypt by Dr George Hart (Macdonald Young Books);

An Introduction to Egyptology by James Putnam (Grange Books).

What you need and preparation

Prepare simple sentences in a language or preferably script that is unknown to the children, for example *Aujourd'hui nous allons à l'école* or a similar sentence written in the script you have found or created. You could use the expertise of the parents of the children in your class to create sentences in other languages, such as Bengali, Yoruba or Serbo-Croat. Write up the first sentence on the board before the children arrive – you could put it up under the 'target for the day'. In a reference book, find a hierglyphic alphabet. Copy it out to make a poster. Gather together images of scribes, their tools and of scribes at work from primary sources (enough for one between two). Prepare translations of some of the pharaohs' names into hieroglyphs.

Learning objective
Select and combine sources of information.

Lesson organisation
Whole-class discussion followed by pairs activity; plenary.

Vocabulary
scribe
hieroglyph
hieratic script
inscription
text

What to do

Introduction

20 mins Direct the children's attention to the sentence. Ask if anyone can read it for the rest of the class. Ask the children how they can work out what the sentence says if they cannot understand the language or script. Encourage the children to discuss how it might be done. Remind them of any experience they may have already had with codes and code breaking. Write up the same sentence in English under the first. Can the children now work out what the script says?

Show the children how to match up the words. Write up another sentence in script or language that uses the same words in a different order, for example *Aujourd'hui nous allons à l'école* becomes *Nous allons à l'école aujourd'hui*. Ask one of the children to put the second sentence into English. Show the children a third sentence that uses only one or two of the known words, for example *Aujourd'hui on va à la piscine.* Can they work this one out?

Use this as a background to explain the problem facing archaeologists before the discovery of the Rosetta Stone. Tell the children about Champollian's work, bringing out the following points:

● The text on the Rosetta Stone is a decree of the Pharaoh Ptolemy V written in Ancient Greek and two Egyptian scripts, demotic and hieroglyphic.

● Champollian studied other hieroglyphic texts and began to recognise and decipher pharaohs' names.

● There are about 700 characters in hieroglyphs compared to 26 letters in our alphabet.

● It took about two years to create a workable alphabet and grammar for hieroglyphs.

● The knowledge of Coptic (an ancient form of written language that is still used in religious texts) helped Champollian work out the phonetic values of the hieroglyphs while his understanding of Greek helped him identify pictorial characters.

Write the name of one of the pharaohs on the board. Ask the children to use the hieroglyphs on your poster to translate the name into hieroglyphs. Work out two or three on the board.

Ask the children if they think that it would have been easy to learn to read and write hieroglyphs. Who do they think had to learn it. They may suggest pharaohs or priests. Explain about the scribes, the sort of work they did, what tools they used, how long it took to train as a scribe and what sort of power they had.

Development

30 mins Split the children into pairs. Give them a picture of scribes at work. Ask them to give a written description of what they see happening. (See an example in *Find Out About Ancient Egypt* by Philip Steele (Southwater), page 44). Explain that they must include ideas of what they think is happening. They also need to say why they think the role of the scribe was important. Give the children 10 minutes to discuss their ideas and then 20 minutes to complete the task. Explain that both children must complete part of the writing each and that they should decorate their work with some Egyptian patterns or with hieroglyphs.

While the children are working in their pairs speak to different groups. Show them a picture of a scribe. Ask them to explain why they think he should be remembered. Can they think of an epitaph to write on his statue? Collect the children's comments and display them with the picture.

Plenary
Share the children's ideas for an epitaph for the scribe and read out some of the finished pieces of writing.

Differentiation
For less able children, provide additional information to explain the picture if it is difficult to work out what is happening.

Assessing learning outcomes
Can the children use a variety of sources to provide the basis for their writing?

What was life like in the city?
1 hour

Background information
Akhetaten, the city which Akhenaten built at Tell el Amarna, was constructed very swiftly and abandoned just as quickly. After his death it was never lived in as a city again. It has remained to provide archaeologists with some excellent evidence of how the city was laid out and what various buildings were used for. The city of Akheteten had wide avenues with a range of different houses. There were workmen's homes situated up near the tombs that were being built in the eastern cliffs. The workers lived in blocks of small houses with three rooms that opened onto the dusty street. In the suburbs, artisans and craftsmen had larger, single-storey buildings with small courtyards, often with studios or workshops attached. The houses of the more affluent clustered around the centre of the city along two roads that ran parallel to the River Nile. These homes were more like small holdings than town houses – they had cattle stalls, kennels and stables as well as extensive grounds. The houses often had two or more storeys with spacious and airy rooms. Some houses also had bathing rooms and toilets. Most had courtyards with shady trees and ornamental lakes. The houses were whitewashed mud brick and were often decorated with colourful images of nature.

In the centre, the temple of Aten dominated the city and situated close to it, overlooking the Nile, were the royal and administrative buildings, such as the police barracks and records office. Akhenaten could look out of his central palace at the busy quays filled with river traffic. There was a summer palace to the south of the city and a palace with a menagerie in the north. The boundaries of the city were marked by stone stelae that Akhenaten had erected.

Further information about can be found in:
The Boy Pharaoh, Tutankhamun by Noel Steatfeild (Michael Joseph) – contains a plan of an Amarnan house; and at:
www.legolas.org/castle/buildings/Tell_el_Amarna-Private_House.jpg.

What you need and preparation
Enlarge photocopiable pages 143 and 144 for display. You will also need: reference books with information about Egyptian life in general; photocopiable pages 141and 142; individual copies of photocopiable pages 143 and 144.

What to do
30 mins **Introduction**
Read the story on photocopiable pages 141 and 142 to the children. Discuss some of the issues brought up in the story, bringing out the following points:

Learning objectives
Demonstrate knowledge and understanding of characteristic features of past societies and periods.

Lesson organisation
Class discussion followed by pairs activity; plenary

Vocabulary
city
temple
avenue
garden
ornamental lake
market
courtyard
road
hall
suburb
barracks
office
military quarters
sanctuary

- Important officials such as Yahmose lived a life of ease surrounded by their extended family and plenty of servants.
- The role of the women was to run the household and care for the children.
- Houses were designed to combat the rigors of the climate – they had high windows (without glass) to let in the light but keep out strong sunlight, flat roofs which could be used to sleep on in hot weather, and courtyards which were partly covered to provide shade.
- Fruit trees and gardens decorated the grounds of more affluent houses and ornamental ponds were also used to provide fish for the family.
- Food was bought each day at local markets as the hot weather meant that food decayed quickly and could not be stored for long.

Ask the children what impression they have of the house. Show them the plan of the official's house on page 144. Talk about what the different areas were used for. Encourage the children to imagine they are in one of the rooms. Can they describe what they might see? Can they describe how to get from one part of the house to another using the plan? Do they have any idea about what the city was like? How do they know this? Ensure the children refer to the story to justify their answers. Show the children the map of Akhetaten on page 143. Point out the different areas. Show the children pictures of what the buildings may have looked like. Describe walking from the gardens of the palace to the Temple of Aten. What would they pass on the way?

20 mins Development
Split the children into pairs. Give each pair an individual copy of the map or the plan of the house. Question children to ensure that they are able to orientate themselves and recognise the different buildings or parts of the house, for example *What building is next to the temple on the right? Where could I go from the entrance?* Explain to the children that they are to take turns in describing a journey through the city or around the house telling their partner what they see along the way.

After the exercise, ask the children what impression they now have of the house or the city. Can they describe different features?

Follow-up activity
Children could draw a pictorial record of their route, illustrating it with little buildings.

10 mins Plenary
Ask the children to describe a number of routes that you have suggested or to describe the routes they discussed with their partner.

Differentiation

For less able children, provide adult support to produce a group response for a chosen route.

Prepare a number of written routes for those children who may have difficulties in devising one themselves.

Assessing learning outcomes

Can the children recognise different features of the city and explain why these were characteristic of the period?

Benin – an African kingdom

One of the aims of the world study units is to give children a wider global perspective. It is important to present children with alternative viewpoints of world history and to allow them to understand the contributions made to history by other peoples. Children need positive images of civilisations that developed outside and independently of Europe. The world study units allow teachers to introduce children to some ancient civilisations that may be less well known than others. Benin is one of those civilisations.

The Empire of Benin was a West African nation that flowered in the 15th and 16th centuries – around the same time as the Tudor period in Britain. Benin City was the centre of the Empire which grew from a collection of villages in the same general area into a mighty trading power that extended over a large geographical area. It was highly influential in West Africa and established strong trading links with European nations. Benin City existed as a powerful trading centre until it was annexed by the British in the 19th century. Benin City lies in the south-east of present-day Nigeria above the River Benue. (It should not be confused with the country of Benin, formerly the French Protectorate of Dahomey, which is situated next to Nigeria.)

While providing a fascinating study in its own right, Benin also allows valuable comparisons to be made with the Tudor period in British history. Both societies revolved around absolutist monarchs: the Tudors in England and the Obas in Benin. Both societies were motivated by the desire to extend their zones of influence through investigating and developing new trade routes. For both, religion was a central and fundamental theme in the lives of the people. In England, Henry VIII consolidated his power by announcing himself Supreme Head of the Church of England. In Benin, the Oba (the chief) claimed a direct link to the gods. His central role was religious and his life was defined by elaborate religious rituals and ceremonies.

The Oba was the pivot of society in Benin. His word was law and there was no appeal against his decisions. The Oba was thought to be descended directly from the gods and the role passed from father to son. The Oba was seen as a magical being who needed no food, drink or sleep. He was constantly attended by priests and medicine men who brewed potions to preserve and strengthen his spiritual powers. The Oba's welfare was paramount as he represented the soul of the land. While he was well and healthy all would go well for the people. No one except the most powerful chiefs spoke directly to the Oba – all conversations were through intermediaries – which the European traders found very frustrating.

Trade was the seat of the Oba's power. Through a sophisticated system of tolls and tributes, the Oba controlled the Empire's trade and so built up his own wealth and power. The Benins carefully regulated European trade by controlling access to the trade road and so to the coast, by setting specific quotas on some commodities and by forbidding the trade of other goods. Some luxury goods belonged exclusively to the Oba, such as coral and ivory. This contributed greatly to his wealth. Trade with the Europeans was conducted on an equal footing, unlike that of the Native Americans who traded glass beads with Columbus. Benin was a strong, effective Empire that had commodities it was prepared to trade with enterprising European merchants.

Our knowledge of this ancient civilisation, as with many others, rests on the work of archaeologists and historians. We have some contemporary accounts from European travellers, but no written accounts from the Benin themselves. This is because Benin was an oral society – its history, laws and customs were transmitted by word of mouth. To find physical evidence of the society, we are dependent on artefacts, such as the Benin bronzes, and archaeological excavations. It is important that the children understand both the importance of the spoken word and storytelling within an oral culture and the work of archaeologists in piecing together the past and making sense of the fragmentary clues they find.

Benin is a colourful topic which allows children to investigate one of the influential African nations of the past. It is an important challenge to stereotypic views that African society was simple and unsophisticated.

UNIT: Benin – an African kingdom

Enquiry questions	Learning objectives	Teaching activities	Learning outcomes	Literacy links	Cross-curricular links
Where, when and why did the Benin Empire develop?	● Give reasons for and results of main events. ● Be aware that the past is divided into different periods.	Teacher-led discussion places the Empire in time and place. Groups use information about geography and trade to explain the Empire's development.	Children: ● give three factors that encouraged the growth of the Empire ● mark Empire on timeline and map	Label diagram and maps to show importance of trade routes. Collect specific vocabulary to link with topic.	Geography: explain how settlements differ and change, using appropriate geographical vocabulary and a variety of maps.
How did the Europeans encounter the Empire?	● Select and combine information from different sources.	Watch *Eureka* video (Trade in the past). Investigation of written accounts and pictorial evidence.	● use the sources to explain how the Europeans and the Benin felt about each other	Write account of what the Europeans and the Benin thought about each other.	Citizenship: be aware of the values and customs of people living in different times.
What was the city like?	● Find answers that go beyond simple observations to make deductions.	Groups use accounts of the city to decide what it was like.	● describe the city based on different accounts ● draw an impression of the city	Write and illustrate an account of the city as if they were writing a report for other travellers.	Art: create a 3-D representation of Benin City using contemporary accounts and a variety of media.
Who was the Oba?	● Demonstrate factual knowledge and understanding of the main people.	Pairs examine evidence from Benin brasses. Teacher-led discussion to expand ideas about position of the Oba.	● explain who the Oba was and why he was important	Use writing frame to note initial impressions and then build up to factual account.	Art: use Benin brasses as a basis for sketching/close observational drawing.
What was life like at the court?	● Recognise similarities and differences between periods in the past.	Groups compare and contrast different aspects of court life with that of the Tudors (such as warriors, hunting, music, role of women).	● contribute to a class display on the similarities and differences in Tudor court and that of Benin	Revise and extend work on note taking by using research materials as a basis for written report.	ICT: use word processing skills to share and exchange information in the form of a poster.
What was the market like?	● Communicate findings in a variety of ways.	Teacher input on the guild system (relate to that of Britain). Pupils research characters for a market scene drama.	● use their research to describe their character in terms of appearance, age and occupation	Write a descriptive character sketch. Use adjectives and focus on small details.	ICT: Create card on programme such as *Hyperstudio* using text, image and sound.
What was life like in a village?	● Select and combine information from sources.	Teacher-led instruction to look at the importance of farming and types of farm product.	● use a variety of sources to write an account of village life.	Write a poem based on imagined experiences.	Geography: contrast farming in modern Nigeria with that of Benin.
Why was storytelling important?	● Show how the past has been represented and interpreted in different ways.	Tell a traditional story using the traditional openings and endings. Discuss the function of storytelling and why it was an important feature of life in Benin.	● demonstrate their understanding of the story by retelling it in a variety of ways	Investigate British and African proverbs. Look at how they work and make a collection from both traditions.	PE dance: create dances using a movements from different times and places (for example West Africa).
What happened to Emotan and Eware?	● Describe some of the main people within a period.	Watch *Eureka* video for the story of Eware. Read additional accounts. Storyboard main events.	● select events from Eware's life to explain what his life was like	Use the Eware story as a basis for writing a playscript.	Citizenship: discuss the issues in the story.
How do we know about Benin's past?	● Evaluate sources of information and identify those that are useful for particular tasks.	Explain oral history tradition. What else can be used to find out about ancient civilisations? Archaeology: groups examine archaeological evidence.	● describe the benefits and limitations of the different types of evidence.	Understand and use the terms 'fact' and 'opinion' and begin to distinguish them through evaluation of sources.	Science: relate properties to the everyday uses of materials; begin to consider the effect of age on different materials.

1 hour Where, when and why did the Benin Empire develop?

Background information

One of the most important factors for the growth of the Benin Empire was the importance of trade and its ability to control that trade. This is one of the main themes of this unit. There were a number of factors that contributed to the growth of this civilisation in that time and place. Firstly, the physical features surrounding the original settlement gave it good natural defences. Benin City was situated on a low-lying plain covered with clear red sand. Behind it stood the tropical rainforest that formed a deep, almost impassable barrier. Hills surrounded the town on all sides except the south, which was protected by swamps. Traders travelled from the coast up river to the port of Guatun. From here a broad earth road wound through the swamps to the city. This secure, defensive position allowed Benin to develop without fear of invasion from other areas.

Secondly, Benin was an important trader in the area, having many goods to trade and the ability to control the local trade. Benin had a well-established trade network that stretched through the rainforest to the desert traders of the Sahara, as well as linking up with other West African kingdoms along the coast. A rich variety of resources from salt to precious metal, slaves to cloth were traded back and forth. Benin controlled the trade routes and the trade that passed along it. Its geographical location also gave the Benin control over access to the coast. This power enabled them to force traders to pay tributes to the Oba.

The third reason for the growth of the civilisation was the aggressive nature of the Empire. Benin had a powerful army and was prepared to use it to control its neighbours and to extract tribute from them, thereby further building up its own power base.

Further information can be found in: *Benin, An African Kingdom* (pack) by Cathy Midwinter (WWF UK); *Eureka – Benin, An African Kingdom (A Teachers' Guide)* by Cathy Midwinter (Educational Television Company); *Benin – Source Pack for Key Stage 2* (Northhamptonshire Black History Group, Wellingborough REC); *The Kingdom of Benin in the Sixteenth Century* by Elizabeth M McClelland (Oxford University Press); *Benin* by Kit Elliott (Cambridge University Press).

This study unit is well supported by resources produced for the Channel 4 television programme, *Eureka – Benin, An African Kingdom*. If you are going to study Benin it would be worth the investment to obtain the resource pack that supports this television series.

What you need and preparation

Find a clear map of present-day West Africa. You will also need individual copies of photocopiable pages 145, 146 and 147, and enlarged copies of photocopiable page 146. For extra reference, see also *The Kingdom of Benin in the Sixteenth Century* by Elizabeth M McClelland, (Oxford University Press). Draw a timeline on the board.

Learning objectives
• Give a few reasons for, and results of, the main events and changes.
• Show an awareness that the past is divided into different periods of time.

Lesson organisation
Teacher-led, whole-class discussion; group investigation of sources followed by individual recording activity.

Vocabulary
Benin City
empire
coast
swamp
tropical rainforest
trade route
river delta
civilisation
traders
influential
settlement
siting

What to do

(30 mins) Introduction

Show the children the timeline. Using the bottom of the timeline, add the periods of British history that the children are familiar with. Point out the Tudors on the timeline. Explain that this is the period of time that they will be looking at. Tell the children what was happening in Britain at this time. Bring out the following points:

● England was just emerging from a period of civil war and was in desperate need of stability.

● A strong dynasty, the Tudors, was just about to take control of the country.

● It was a time of great exploration and discovery in terms of ideas and physical exploration of the world.

● New cultures were being continually encountered.

● Trade and the need to find new trade routes was fuelling this exploration and expansion.

The children may already have looked at the Tudors and so this unit can be used as a revision and consolidation of the period. Alternatively, they may be going to study the period later in the key stage. This unit can then form an introduction to a more detailed study at a later date.

Ask the children if they know what was happening in the rest of the world at this time. They may have heard of the Aztec or Mayan civilisations or the Renaissance period (through the art curriculum or 'Famous people' at Key Stage 1). Add these periods to the timeline. What do the children think was happening in India, Japan or in other African states? It is important to combat the stereotypical conception that Europe was the only 'civilised' place at this period.

Once you have established that there were other important civilisations flourishing at this time you can introduce Benin. Use the top of the timeline to give background information about the development of the Empire and how and when it encountered the Europeans. Show where the period would come on a wider timeline and consider how long ago the period was. Bring out the following points:

● Trade was the reason why the Europeans were exploring the coast of West Africa. They were looking for resources and some way to circumnavigate the influence of the Muslim control of Mediterranean trade routes.

● Benin was already established as a power in the region and as a strong, influential Empire before the Europeans arrived.

● Europe and Benin met on equal terms, both having items they wanted to trade.

Help the children to place the civilisation geographically as well as in time. Show the children the map of West Africa and enlarged version of photocopiable page 145. Locate the site of Benin on them for the children. What do they notice about where it was situated?

Give out copies of photocopiable page 146. Look for clues to decide why the site was beneficial. Ask the children what they need to consider, for example defence, lines of communication, natural material. Discuss the physical aspects of the site. Why might they be important? How might they affect the development of civilisation? Collate their answers on the board.

(20 mins) Development

Hand out individual copies of photocopiable page 145. Split the children into groups. Ask the groups to work together, using the information they have already gained as well as the information on the map, to answer the questions below.

● What were the main resources that were being traded?

● Where were the different resources coming from?

● What resources did Benin have to offer the Europeans in trade and where did these resources come from?

● How did Benin's position help its development?

● What else could Benin do to develop trade further?

 Plenary
10 mins Ask a representative from each group to feed back what they have discovered to the whole class. Collate the answers on the board. Answer any questions that the children were unable to. Can the children now explain how the geographical location of Benin contributed to the development of the civilisation in that time and that place?

Differentiation
Children can be organised into mixed-ability groups for the group activity.

Assessing learning outcomes
Can the children give three factors that encouraged the growth of the Empire? Can they mark the Empire on the timeline and map?

Follow-up activity
Ask the children to fill in photocopiable page 147.

What was the city like?
1 hour 10 mins

Background information
The first Europeans who arrived at the city of Benin were impressed and surprised by its size and splendour. The city was heavily fortified with huge, thick, mud walls. Around the outside of the city ran at least two wide dry ditches, called iya. The height of the fortifications was about 17.5m from the bottom of the iya to the top of the wall. It seems probable that the walls were constructed over at least a couple of dry seasons – the number of people needed to complete the task in one season would have been huge (around 5000 or so). Large, heavily guarded, wooden gates opened into the main street of the city. Lanes and streets ran off from the central thoroughfare bordered by houses with high walls made of red mud. Houses of the rich had a series of courtyards and semi-thatched rooms that led off from a main door which was reached by two or three steps from the road. The walls of the houses were about half a metre thick and were polished to a high gloss by the women who rubbed the walls with wet cloths and the shells of giant land snails! Inside, the rooms were decorated with brightly coloured, woven wall hangings and the benches and beds were covered with raffia mats.

As in many tropical areas, people lived in the open air for much of the time. Extended families tended to live close together as they often had a shared craft or profession. This meant that different parts of the city were home to different guilds or crafts. The colour, noise and bustle of the city was attractive to many of the European visitors. They remarked, in contemporary accounts, on the busy life that went on around them. However, it should be remembered that these accounts were written by Europeans and are not particularly reliable. Some of the writers were trying to make sense of what they were seeing; the writers of some accounts had not actually visited the country!

Written and pictorial contemporary sources can be found in:
Benin, An African Kingdom (Pack) by Cathy Midwinter (WWF UK); *Benin – Source Pack for Key Stage 2,* (Northhamptonshire Black History Group, Wellingborough REC); *The Kingdom of Benin in the Sixteenth Century* by Elizabeth M McClelland (Oxford University Press); *Benin* by Kit Elliott (Cambridge University Press).

What you need and preparation
Gather together a selection of contemporary written accounts of Benin City. Find a copy of Olfert Dapper's engraving of Benin. Create a report sheet (see page 12). You will also need: photocopiable page 148 – enough for one per child; *Eureka* television series on Benin, if available.

Learning objective
Find answers from sources that go beyond simple observations to make deductions.

Lesson organisation
Whole-class introduction followed by group activity; whole-class plenary.

Vocabulary
fortifications
ditch
moat
city
thatch
courtyards
thoroughfare
wards
partitions

What to do

(20 mins) Introduction

Tell the children about the city of Benin. Ask them what they think the city was like. Encourage the children to use their own experiences of cities to try to come to some conclusions. They may mention things such as crowded streets, lots of houses. They may suggest something about the weather or geographical features linked to the previous session. They may have some idea about Tudor London and make reference to this. If the television programme is available they could watch the relevant section. How true a representation do the children think the television programme was? How can they find out? What sort of sources would be available and how reliable would they be? What do they think the people would use to build their homes and where would they get this from?

Note down some of the impressions that the children have, and encourage them to justify their answers.

Explain to the children that they must work as a group to examine some contemporary sources and decide what sort of impressions they give us of ancient Benin.

(40 mins) Development

Split the children into groups and pair them up within each group. Give each pair a copy of photocopiable page 148 and the report sheet. Ask them to discuss one of the sources and use it to complete their report sheet. Ask one child from each pair to report back to the rest of the class what they have found out about Benin City from their source. *Are there any differences in the accounts?* Ask the children what could have caused this. *What effect does this have on our perceptions of the city? Are there any sources that are liable to be more reliable that others?*

Ask each group to create a poster that gives their findings using text diagrams, sketch maps and pictorial impressions. Tell them to focus on four or five features in detail, for example the layout of the roads, the height of the walls and so on. Ask them to draw pictures of what they think the city was like. Explain that each person in the group should contribute something to the poster.

(10 mins) Plenary

Ask each group in turn to show their poster to the rest of the class. Ask the class if there are any points that are common to all the posters. Are there different features on the posters?

Show the children Olfert Dapper's engraving of Benin. Ask the children how true they think Dapper's picture is to the real city of Benin. Why do they think this? Explain to the children that Dapper had never been to Benin. Ask the children to complete sentences on the board such as, *We think Olfert's picture is... We think this is because...*

Direct the children's attention back to their group's poster. Ask them if they think they have made a better use of the sources and created a truer representation of Benin.

Differentiation

Sort text by level of difficulty. Transcribe the sources into simpler text if necessary. Provide a pictorial vocabulary sheet for less able groups. Provide adult support for less able groups to help with structuring the activity.

Ask more able children to research the palace of the Oba. Tell them to write an account of what it could have been like and draw a picture or diagram. Direct them towards the Internet to help them with their research.

Assessing learning outcomes

Can the children describe the city based on the different accounts? Can they draw an impression of the city from the accounts?

ICT opportunities
Use a desktop publishing programme to edit and refine the text used on the posters.

Follow-up activities
• Create a class display with posters.
• Include contemporary illustration and the evaluation of that source.

(50 mins) Who was the Oba?

Background information

The Oba was the supreme ruler of Benin. Like the Ancient Egyptian pharaohs, he was both god and king to his subjects. His word was law and no one would gainsay his decisions. The Oba was supposed to have supernatural powers, needing neither food nor drink, nor ever sleeping. An atmosphere of awe and dread surrounded him. The Oba in his palace was the centre of the kingdom. The palace was enormous – the size of a small town. It was the Oba's dwelling place, the centre of government, a religious centre and the military headquarters. It was a sprawling collection of rooms and courtyards with three separate elements. In one part lived those who looked after the Oba's wardrobe and regalia, in another were those who were responsible for his harem and their children. In the last section lived the Oba and the servants who looked after his personal comfort. The Oba was also surrounded by craftsmen and women, noblemen, soldiers, musicians and huntsmen.

The Oba was an impressive figure who was rarely seen outside the confines of his palace. He was dressed from head to waist in red coral – coral being sacred as well as a sign of rank. The costume was so heavy that he had to be supported by arm-bearers who held the Oba up by supporting his arms. He also wore a pointed crown of coral with fringes of coral and coral necklaces encircled his neck. He had huge ivory and bronze bangles around his arms. An enormous cotton skirt hid his legs and feet as it was believed that an earlier Oba had fish instead of feet!

The Oba was surrounded by other symbols of his wealth and rank such as servants carrying the execution swords and spears and leading the royal leopards. No one spoke to him directly but had to address their remarks to one of his attendant chiefs.

What you need and preparation

Enlarge photocopiable page 149 for display, or copy it onto an acetate for use on the OHP. On a flip chart, board or OHT, draw three columns with the headings: *Words to describe the Oba, Why do you think this? What do you think now?* You will also need: photocopiable pages 150–151 – enough for the children to share one between two. If possible, gather together primary source images of Benin brasses that show the Oba.

What to do

(20 mins) Introduction

Explain to the children that where they had previously used written accounts as sources of information they will now be concentrating on pictorial sources. These are important because they give evidence from the point of view of the people of Benin of themselves and their Oba. Show the children the large image of the Oba. Explain to them who the Oba was.

Ask the children to look carefully at the picture and talk about what sort of impression it gives them of the Oba.

Ask the children to think of four or five words that describe what they think about the picture. Write the words in each box in the first column you have prepared on the board or on the OHP.

Learning objective
Demonstrate factual knowledge and understanding of the main people of the period.

Lesson organisation
Pairs activity; whole-class plenary; follow-up.

Vocabulary
Oba
royalty
palace
supernatural
government
regalia
servants
coral
ivory
bronze
crown
bangle
symbol
wealth
rank
sword
spear
ceremonial
costume

Ask the children to justify their choices. Collate their answers on the second column of the grid. The grid should begin to look as follows:

Words to describe the Oba	Why do you think this?	What do you think now?
scary	He has staring eyes.	
strong	He is holding cats in each hand.	

 Development

Split the children into pairs. Give each pair a copy of photocopiable pages 149 and 150. Explain to the children that they should work together to describe what they see in the picture, for example, *There is a man holding two cats. The man is wearing a hat and a dress. The background is patterned with flowers.* Ask the children to fill in the first two columns of the grid on page 150.

10 **Plenary**
mins Bring the children back together and ask some of them to feed back their results. What have they found out? What sort of impression do the children have of the Oba? Was he an important person or not? Why do they think this?

Return to the original picture. Give the children some of the background information and explain the symbolism of the picture. Tell them that the cats are in fact leopards – a symbol of royalty. The leopards were seen as having the power of the forest and they symbolised the Oba's power in the kingdom. The hat and dress are ceremonial costume and are made of coral – they demonstrate his wealth and importance as coral had to be imported. The mudfish lived on land and in the sea – they symbolise how the Oba controls both land and sea. Large eyes were seen as a sign of beauty. The sword was a symbol of the Oba's authority over his subjects. As you give the children this information, go back to the grid and fill in the last column. The grid should now look like this:

Give the children a copy of photocopiable page 151, and ask them to fill in their third column,

Words to describe the Oba	Why do you think this?	What do you think now?
scary	He has staring eyes.	Large eyes are a sign of beauty.
strong	He is holding cats in each hand.	He can control leopards so he must be powerful.

working in pairs. They should also complete the statement: *We think that the Oba was/was not important because…*

Differentiation
Simplified text and adult support could be given to less able children. Less able children could also work as a group with adult support, rather than in pairs.

ICT opportunities
Use an art program to create a sheet of paper with a simple repeat pattern, based on the patterns used on the Benin Brasses, scattered over the page. Use the paper to present the written or word-processed descriptive writing about the Oba.

Assessing learning outcomes
Can the children explain who the Oba was and why he was important?

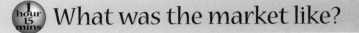

What was the market like?

Background information
Trade was the source of Benin's power. The geographical position of the Empire between the sea and the vast interior meant that Benin controlled important trade routes. These led in two main directions: to the coast, and inland and up country northwards (see photocopiable page 145). The coastal trade was mainly with the Europeans, while inland, Benin traded with other African kingdoms. The Oba rigidly controlled trading rights and kept a monopoly on some types of goods such as palm oil, ivory and slaves.

There were two markets in Benin City and they were held every four days. Farmers and huntsmen came from the forest and women potters carried their merchandise in from the surrounding villages. White-gowned Arab traders brought goods from the northern routes, tracing produce back to the camel caravans that crossed the Sahara from the Mediterranean. Europeans came up river from Guatun. The place thronged with noise and colour and a vast variety of goods was on sale. Markets lasted all day and each vendor had their own allotted space with a little stall made by large mats suspended over four upright poles. Traders from the North brought dried fish, salt, pepper and blue Benin cloth. Important local industries were ivory carving and brass casting. European traders brought cloth, guns and trinkets such as looking glasses and penknives to bargain with. Trade was mainly barter but brass manillas and cowrie shells were used as currency.

Merchants and traders were organised into guilds, much as they were in medieval and Tudor England. Crafts were usually learned from parents and passed down through families. Often groups of guilds became linked with one group supplying the other. Each craft had its own area of town.

More source material can be found in:

'The Empire', 'Society and Industry' – Benin, Source Pack for Key Stage 2;

'Trade and Markets' – Benin, an African Kingdom.

What you need and preparation
Photocopiable pages 152–3; individual copies of photocopiable pages 154, 155 and 156 (enough for each child to have one of them); further source material on Benin markets made into packs. You will also need: props such as baskets, pots, brass manillas (made of twisted foil paper) and shells (cowries if possible) and so on. You may also want to arrange for the use of a larger space, such as the hall, for the market scene.

What to do

30 mins Introduction
Read the story on photocopiable pages 152–3 to the class. Explain any unknown vocabulary to the children and question them to see if there are any elements of the story that they do not understand.

Ask the children about their impressions of the story. Ensure that you ask a mixture of open as well as closed questions, for example, What happens to Osasere? What does her father do? What is the market like? What else does she see in the market? What does she think of the Europeans and why does she think this?

Encourage the children to justify their answers by refering back to the text.

Explain specific features of Benin society raised by the story, such as how a guild worked, what a barter system meant and how the market might have been organised.

Learning objectives
• Select and combine information from sources.
• Communicate findings in a variety of ways.

Lesson organisation
Whole-class, teacher-led discussion; individual research task; group activity.

Vocabulary
market
trader
merchant
trade route
craftsmen
craftswomen
potter
ironworker
ivory carver
brass casting
guild
merchandise
vendor
brass manilla
cowrie shell

Development

25 mins Explain that the children are going to research characters from the Benin market and then act out their characters as part of a role-play about the market. Keep a central role for yourself, perhaps as the manager of the market. Introduce your character to the children so that they have some idea of what they need to do.

Split the class into three groups: vendors, Europeans and buyers. Hand out the appropriate photocopiable page 154, 155 or 156 to each group.

Give each group a pack of source material and selection of pictures if any are available. Pictures of modern African markets can also be used here to help children visualise the scene. Explain to the children that they must decide what sort of characters they will be and then use the sources to build up a picture of their character. Give the children 15 minutes to discuss and research their characters, either individually or with adult support. Then tell the children to spend 10 minutes making some written notes on their photocopiable pages.

While this is happening you or another adult can be setting up a large area that will become the market.

Plenary

20 mins Role-play – Benin market in the 16th century. Explain to the children that the classroom or hall is now the main market of Benin City. In your role as the market manager, open the market and allow the children to start to set up their stalls. After a few minutes, allow the Europeans to enter the market. Children can role-play what happens when they arrive.

ICT opportunities
Create a card on a mutimedia program such as *Hyperstudio* using text, image and sound.

Differentiation

Children who have difficulty writing can have simplified texts and could record their notes on a tape recorder rather than writing them down.

Assessing learning outcomes

Can the children use their research to describe their character in terms of age, physical appearance, occupation and purpose for being in the market?

1 hour Why was storytelling important?

Learning objective
Show how the past has been represented and interpreted in different ways.

Lesson organisation
Whole-class storytelling session; group work to retell session using music and dance (additional time will be needed to work on and then perform pieces).

Background information

Until the 20th century, the Benin language of Edo was a spoken language only and, as in many other oral societies, storytelling was an important feature of people's lives. Stories helped children understand their history by explaining how things had happened in the past, for example how the country came to be. Through these shared stories and experiences, children came to develop a strong sense of identity. The oral transmission of official history was an important element of court procedure. Official storytellers at the court held details of the deeds of past Obas and complicated genealogies in their heads as they did in many other societies with an oral tradition (such as Maoris and ancient Celtic kingdoms).

Storytelling was an integral part of family life. Central areas within the home provided space for people to gather as a family or with their friends and neighbours to share storytelling sessions. Traditional forms for opening and closing stories added to the drama. Many of these stories included music or other features such as the use of proverbs. If a professional storyteller was present a traditional musical instrument called an akpata might be used to give emphasis to certain points in the story.

Further information can be found in *Benin, an African Kingdom* by Cathy Midwinter (WWF UK) – 'The Oral Tradition – Oral histories, storytelling and proverbs'. Examples of traditional stories can be found in the above source and in *Benin, an African Kingdom,* 'The Storybook', retold by Deborah Isaacs and Elizabeth Isaacs (The Educational Television Company).

What you need and preparation

Learn the story on photocopiable pages 157–8. It is best to learn the story so that you can tell it rather than read it as it will be more effective this way. Learn the traditional opening and closing phrases. Arrange the classroom in such a way that it is conducive to storytelling and creating an atmosphere. You may want to book the hall or use the library. You may want to dress in a traditional robe. Ensure that the children are sitting comfortably at your feet. Children should have had time to experiment with some African instruments such as gatto drums and cabassa. They should also have had time in PE/dance sessions to begin to investigate or experiment with traditional African dance and movement.

What to do

25 mins **Introduction**

Settle the children to listen to the story by sitting on the floor around the storyteller. Teach the children the responses they should make. Open the storytelling by using the traditional opening. Encourage the children to make the response and then the story can begin.

Tell your version of the story of Eware and the Portraits of Bronze, making it as colourful and effective as you can – take the bones of the story and embellish it. Make the most of your voice. You could also use a musical instrument to add emphasis to your tale. Close the story with the traditional ending.

Give the children a little time to think about the story. Ask them if they enjoyed it and what they liked best about it. Ask the children about the main points of the story. Question them to see which points they felt were most important. These may be different depending on the child. Pick out and discuss some of these points. Explain to the children about the importance of oral history. Talk about how stories were transmitted by a variety of people, travelling tellers of tales, official court bards, different members of the family. Some stories were very long and complicated but people learned to listen very carefully and so could remember them after hearing them only once. Important events and famous people were remembered through the stories told about them rather than in any written histories.

Ask the children:
● If you were to tell the story using music or dance, how would you show some of these points?
● How would you sequence the story?
● Would you try to tell all of the story or just part of it?

25 mins **Development**

Explain to the children that they are going to retell the story using music or dance. Split the children into groups (ensure that there is sufficient room available for children to begin to work on their sequence of movements).

Give each group a different scene from the story to work on. Explain to the children that each group must create a dance to tell their part of the story, selecting the elements themselves that they want to show. They can work either with movement alone or accompanied by music, depending on the availability of instruments.

 Plenary
At the end of the session, ask each group to show part of their dance to the rest of the class. Continue to develop sequences in PE sessions.

Differentiation
Children will need adult support in structuring the task depending on their confidence and previous experience with this type of work.

Assessing learning outcomes
Can the children demonstrate their understanding of the story by retelling it in a variety of ways?

**ICT
opportunities**
Video work on different pieces. Use it to modify dance. Video the final performance as a record.

How do we know about Benin's past?

**Learning
objective**
Evaluate sources of information and identify those that are useful for particular tasks.

**Lesson
organisation**
Teacher-led discussion; group activity; whole-class plenary.

Vocabulary
archaeology
archaeologist
evidence
excavation

Background information
It is important that children understand the place of oral history and how it functions within an oral society. It is also important that they understand that it gives an account from the point of view of the people themselves. Written accounts may be biased as they are often written by those of another culture. On the other hand, oral history may include elements of myth and legend as people strive to explain their past. There may also be a political bias or events may be remembered wrongly.

Different sources provide different types of evidence. Children need to be able to compare the different types of evidence and reflect on what they reveal. It is also important when considering the work of archaeologists to remember that they may have particular theories they want to prove and that their evidence can be used in a variety of ways.

The main archaeological evidence for Benin comes from the excavations of the city and especially the city walls. Details of this archaeological evidence can be found in: *Benin, an African Kingdom* by Cathy Midwinter (WWF UK), 'People and the environment', 'City and Village life', 'Society and Industry'; *Benin, Source Pack for Key Stage 2.*

What you need and preparation
If possible, arrange for an archaeologist to visit the class and explain what is meant by the study of archaeology and what types of skills are used. Local museums can put you in touch with local archaeological societies and most counties have an archaeology team. Gather together reference material describing archaeological digs on the site of Benin along with examples of other evidence such as pictures of Benin brasses, artefacts and written accounts. You will also need: individual copies of photocopiable pages 159–60.

What to do
20 **Introduction**
Remind the children of any Benin stories you have covered with them. This could be the story of Eware and Emotan (see the grid on page 80). Question them about the factual nature of the story. Were there any elements of the story that seemed strange/unusual/unlikely to them? *Is this a true story? How can we know if this is a true story or not?* Children may mention physical

evidence such as Emotan's statue, if you have used this story. They may think of written accounts they have studied or the pictorial evidence such as Benin brasses. Do the children think that it is necessary to have other evidence to support the oral history?

Introduce the children to the work of the archaeologist. Make links to such sources as Channel 4's *Time Team* programme or archaeological discoveries such as Troy or Tutankhamun's tomb. Ask them:

● What do archaeologists do?

● What problems do they encounter?

Tell the children about the role of archaeologists, bringing out the following points:

● Archaeologists rarely have the whole picture. They have to try to put information together to understand the evidence that has been left.

● Much of the evidence that archaeologists work with is that which has been discarded such as the contents of a refuse heap!

● Archaeology is painstaking, detailed and scientific.

● Technology such as geothermic surveys are increasingly able to aid understanding but much evidence is still found by people digging through the earth by hand.

(30 mins) Development

Split the class into groups. Give each group a picture of the walls of Benin City or a picture of an artefact or a written account of an excavation. Hand out copies of photocopiable pages 159–60. Explain to the children that they are going to be investigating how much information about Benin they can gather from their 'evidence'. Are there any problems or deficiencies with their evidence? Ask the children to fill in the first set of questions on photocopiable pages 159–60 using the source material they have been given.

Give the groups 10 minutes with their 'evidence' then swap the sources around the groups. Ask the children to record their observations on the second source on their record sheet. After 10 minutes swap the sources around again so that each group has 10 minutes with a third source.

(10 mins) Plenary

Bring the groups back together to discuss their findings. What have they discovered? Were there any types of evidence that were better than others? Were there any that gave information for one area but not another? Was any piece of evidence sufficient by itself or did they all need to be corroborated in some way? How important is the work of the archaeologist in making sense of the past? Remind the children of the points made earlier of how archaeologists put together small clues from a variety of sources to create a larger picture.

Assessing learning outcomes

Can the children describe the benefits and limitations of different types of evidence?

Follow-up activity
If possible, arrange a class visit to the British Museum (London) to allow children to see artefacts or some of the Benin brasses.

PHOTOCOPIABLE

ROMANS, ANGLO-SAXONS AND VIKINGS: The Romans

Who lived in Britain before the Romans? Page 10

The coming of the Romans

Beric awoke to unusual sounds. Men were shouting and running about, ponies were stamping and snorting. He opened his eyes. As usual the first thing he saw was the great cone of the thatched roof above him, hung with smoky cobwebs. He rolled over to look at the wood fire in the centre of the roundhouse, where his mother should have been crouched cooking bannocks for his breakfast. The fire was a low mound of ashes glowing orange in the middle. She had not even put more wood on it yet! Beric threw off his blanket and rolled off the pile of sheepskins. He pulled on his clothes and ran outside.

Beric's roundhouse was one of five in the farmstead. His was the biggest. If you stood with your back to the far wall and walked right across, it took twenty paces (except you had to go round the fire in the middle). Grandfather, father, mother, Uncle Cradoc, Auntie Bronwen, Beric and his sister Gwen all lived there. Other uncles and their families lived in two of the other huts and the other two huts were for storing farm equipment. The houses were arranged in a circle with an open space in the middle. A wooden stockade surrounded the farmstead, with two gates in it.

This morning the enclosure was filled with people and ponies. Beric's stomach churned with excitement when he saw what was standing outside his house. Two beautiful, copper-red ponies with bright bronze studs and ornaments on their harness were hitched to a low, light, war chariot. A young

man stood in it holding the reins proudly, while its owner stood behind him shouting orders to everyone. Beric did not know the chief in the chariot but he knew from the golden torc around his neck that it must be one of the sons of Buodoc, King of the Dobunni.

"Beric, don't stand there like a fool – run and harness White Star," said Beric's father's suddenly as he bustled past Beric, carrying his spear, while his mother tagged along behind desperately trying to buckle on his swordbelt for him. Beric ran for the harness and hurried to find his father's favourite pony.

ROMANS, ANGLO-SAXONS AND VIKINGS: The Romans
Who lived in Britain before the Romans? Page 10

PHOTOCOPIABLE

Three hours later, Beric was still excited but he was scared as well. Along the old track to the sea a long column of the Dobunni war band moved. First came the great men in their chariots. There was one woman warrior among them too. Then came the farmers like Beric's father, riding their ponies with their wood and bronze shields slung on their backs. Young relations and slaves trotted along beside their leaders, carrying spears. Beric was still a bit angry that he had not been allowed to bring one of his father's hunting spears. "You are coming as a messenger, not a warrior, this time," his father had insisted. "I promised your mother."

When the fight came, two days later, Beric saw it all from the top of a tree where his father had left him. "Watch what happens – if I can't come back, run home and tell them. Look after your mother and sister."

The battle was not how battles should be. The chiefs of the Dobunni charged out in their chariots, their chests blue with war patterns painted with woad. Their hair flew in the wind as they shouted challenges to the heroes of the Roman army to come out and fight them. But no heroes came. Just a wall of square shields moving forward all together like one great animal, clanking slowly and steadily on. The chiefs were too proud to fight common men so they moved back. The main army of the Dobunni left their ponies and ran forward, screaming war cries. The Roman wall stopped. Just before the Dobunni reached them, a hail of spears flew from the Roman line. Then the line of shields moved forward again, with the short Roman swords chopping and stabbing around them. Crunch, clank, the Roman animal ate the Dobunni war band. Beric found White Star and rode home like the wind.

PHOTOCOPIABLE

ROMANS, ANGLO-SAXONS AND VIKINGS: The Romans
Why did the Romans invade Britain? Page 11

Roman accounts of the Roman invasion of Britain

Claudius only made one invasion and that did not take long. The senate had given him medals but he knew he did not deserve them so he wanted a real Triumph[1]. He chose Britain for this purpose because no one had attacked it since Julius Caesar. One British king was angry with the Romans because they would not send back some of his enemies who had run away across the Channel. Claudius sailed from Ostia to Marseilles and he was nearly shipwrecked in a storm.

Then he marched to Boulogne from where he sailed across to Britain. A part of Britain gave up straight away without a fight and Claudius came home in less than six months. He had his Triumph in Rome and invited everyone to it. Messalina, his wife, followed his chariot in a covered litter. Those who had earned medals in the same war rode behind; the rest followed on foot, wearing robes with the broad stripes. Crassus Frugi was mounted upon a horse with expensive ornaments, in a robe embroidered with palm leaves, because this was the second time he had obtained honours.

From **The Lives of the Twelve Caesars** by Suetonius (born AD75, died AD160). *He was a secretary to the Emperor Hadrian who wrote a History of the Emperors.*

*Triumph: a big military parade through Rome. The Emperor went in front in a chariot. The soldiers marched behind and there would be cartloads of precious things that they had captured and prisoners in chains.

ROMANS, ANGLO-SAXONS AND VIKINGS: The Romans

Why did the Romans invade Britain? Page 11   PHOTOCOPIABLE

After Caesar's wars in Germany it was nearly the end of summer, and he decided to go to Britain. He did this because the British kept sending men to help the Gauls fight against him. Even if it was too late in the year to finish the war before winter, he thought it would be a good idea to go and find out about the country and its people. The Gauls did not seem to know much about it – nobody went to Britain except traders and they only knew about the bits near the sea and near Gaul. He called a lot of traders to talk to him but they did not know how big Britain was or much about the people who lived there. He wanted to know whether they were good fighters, how they lived and where the good places to land his ships were. He sent a captain called Caius Volusenus with a warship to find out what he could…

The British found out from the traders that Caesar was thinking of invading, and some British tribes sent ambassadors to see him. They promised that they would welcome him and become part of the Roman Empire. He promised to help them against their enemies…

From **The Gallic Wars** by Julius Caesar (born 104BC, died 44BC)
Julius Caesar was a Roman general and a politician. He wrote about his own battles to make himself popular.

Caesar used Itium as a base to attack Britain. He set sail at night and got there about four hours after the sun came up. The journey was about 100 km. He saw corn growing in the fields near the coast. Most of Britain is flat and covered with woods and forests, but there are some hills. Britain produces corn, cattle, gold, silver and iron, which are exported. It also sends leather and slaves and good hunting dogs abroad. The Gauls use British dogs, as well as their own, to fight for them in wars.

From **The Geography of Strabo** (born about 45BC, died about AD25)
Strabo was a traveller and geographer. He did not visit Britain but he collected information about it from other writers and travellers.

ROMANS, ANGLO-SAXONS AND VIKINGS: The Romans
What was it like to live in a Roman villa? Page 13

PHOTOCOPIABLE

The Gemini twins

It was a beautiful, bright, cold winter's day and the fields behind the villa glistened with frost. The Gemini, the twins Claudia and Claudius, had two hours of freedom before their tutor called them for lessons. He was a Greek slave called Dion. He had been very expensive because he was so well educated and the twins were expected to be polite to him and treat him almost like a free person. They did not have to be polite to old Beric, he was just a farm slave.

But he was their friend so they were usually nice to him. Anyway, father was very strict and he said that Roman ladies and gentlemen should always have good manners.

Beric was carrying logs to the hypocaust of the winter dining room. They tagged along and watched as he carefully built them up in the fireplace in the outside wall. At first the fire kept blowing smoke out into his face. He fanned it and covered the front with a wooden board until at last it was alight and smoke started to wisp out of the six chimneys around the top of the walls. Now the heat was being drawn under the mosaic floor, and by tonight the dining room would be nice and warm.

"Have you got to do the bathhouse now?" asked Claudia.

"First I will be making ready this room," said Beric. He still spoke Latin with a very strong accent even though he had been a slave since he was a boy.

Beric brought water to wash the mosaic. As he swilled it over, the bright colours came to life. There was a figure meant to be Winter in one corner, holding a bare branch; Summer had an ear of corn and blond hair; Spring was young and dressed in green; Autumn held a bunch of grapes. When the floor was clean, Beric pulled back the couches, where the men would lie down to eat, in a horseshoe shape around one end of the table. The twins helped by setting out the ladies' chairs at the other end.

Father had important guests tonight. A cousin from Rome had been sent to Britannia to join his legion and he was bringing a friend

ROMANS, ANGLO-SAXONS AND VIKINGS: The Romans

What was it like to live in a Roman villa? Page 13

PHOTOCOPIABLE

to dinner. The twins had never been to Rome – they had never been anywhere except Rutupiae, and Londinium once. They hoped that they would be able to stay up and listen to their cousin talk about the great city. The twins chattered on about Rome. Beric nodded and grunted as he worked. He was a good listener. "Now the bathhouse," he said.

The villa was built around three sides of a square courtyard filled with gravel and stone pots for plants. The winter dining room was on the southern corner of the east wing. The baths were right over the other side on the north-west corner. They were quite small ones, just a changing room, a warm room, a hot room and a cold plunge bath. The fire in the bathhouse was very tricky to manage. If you were not careful the hot room was either like an oven or too cold. Beric was an expert and he always got it just right so that the twins' father could relax in his towel and have a good sweat.

"Did your father teach you to make the bathhouse fires?" said Claudius before his sister could kick him to quieten him.

Beric stood up very straight and looked at him. "My father was a warrior," he answered quietly. "Before your people came, he did not carry wood and build fires."

Claudia pulled her brother outside. "Stupid! Don't you remember that Beric's father owned all this land before the invasion? You didn't have to remind him."

"Don't call me stupid. I can't help it if we won, can I?"

A clatter of hooves on the paved road distracted them and they turned to look. "It's cousin Marcus and his friend!" shouted Claudius and ran towards the road, quickly followed by Claudia.

Two fine horses came trotting into sight, ridden by two young men in officers' uniforms. Their helmets shone and their red crests and cloaks blew in the wind.

"Hello, cousin Marcus!" shouted the children.

Beric stood in the doorway of the bathhouse and watched them come. Then the old man turned away and went back to his work.

A plan of a villa

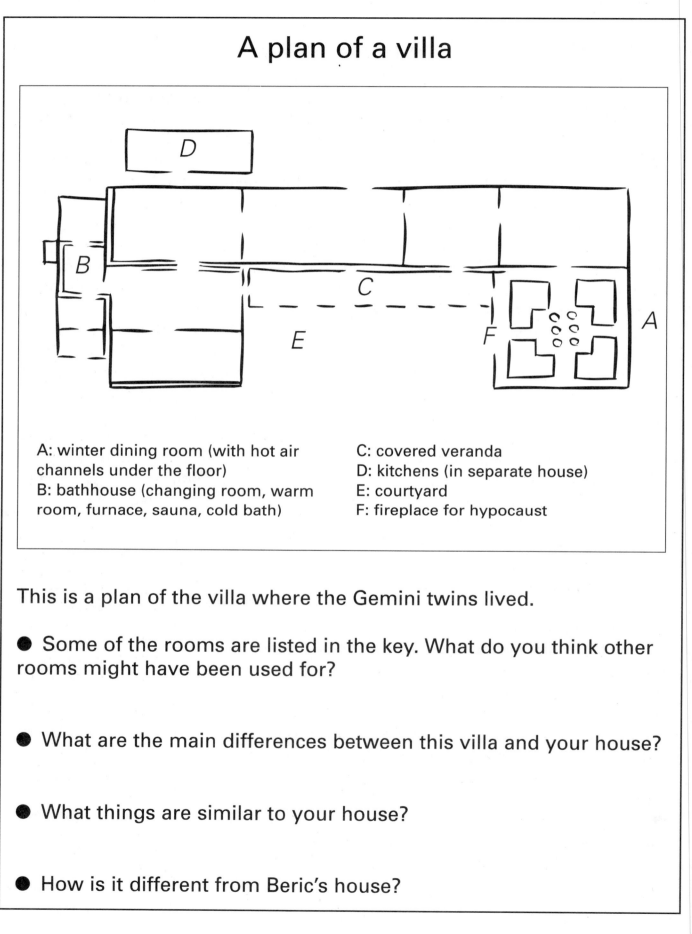

A: winter dining room (with hot air channels under the floor)
B: bathhouse (changing room, warm room, furnace, sauna, cold bath)
C: covered veranda
D: kitchens (in separate house)
E: courtyard
F: fireplace for hypocaust

This is a plan of the villa where the Gemini twins lived.

● Some of the rooms are listed in the key. What do you think other rooms might have been used for?

● What are the main differences between this villa and your house?

● What things are similar to your house?

● How is it different from Beric's house?

ROMANS, ANGLO-SAXONS AND VIKINGS: The Anglo-Saxons
Why did the Anglo-Saxons come to Britain? Page 20

PHOTOCOPIABLE

Witta's story

My name is Witta. I am about 16 years old but already I am a great warrior. I have been in two fights and I would have killed my first man in the last one except that I slipped and fell over when I was chasing him. He was only a farmer anyway, with a pitchfork instead of a spear so I would not have been able to boast much about killing him when the men tell stories after a feast.

I came to this land of Kent six months ago. Before that, I was living across the sea. My father's hall was built on a terp, a mound of earth, because the land often flooded in the winter and the sea came in and covered our fields. Last year the floods were very bad and most of our barley and oats were destroyed before we could cut them. That meant that we had hardly any flour to make bread in the winter and many people died of starvation. In the spring a man came to the Hall. He said that he was a messenger from a great leader called Hengest. He said that Hengest had a war band who worked for a king in Britain called Vortigern. Hengest and his men had to fight against anyone who attacked the king's land; in return they were given Roman gold and good land to farm. Hengest needed more warriors for his band. I jumped up immediately and asked my father's permission to join Hengest. I was tired of being hungry and of sitting on a soggy hill with the sea all around me. Also I wanted a chance to fight and be a warrior. Where I come from only warriors get any respect. As you can see, my father let me go, along with two or three other men.

I remember my first sight of Kent from Hengest's war-boat. There were white cliffs high above the sea and a green beautiful land with hills and trees. The men who met us looked fat and well-fed. I knew that this was the land for me and here I would stay.

I think that there will be war soon. More and more warriors are joining Hengest and many of them want more land to start farms. Sometimes there is trouble with the Romans who live nearby if some of us get drunk and make a little raid on their fancy villas to find gold or something to sell to buy nice ornaments and weapons. We take their women as slaves as we need them to cook and mend our clothes.

Vortigern thinks that he can tell us what to do, but how can we respect people who will not even fight for themselves? Soon we will have to teach Vortigern that we are here to stay.

boast Saxon warriors were expected to boast about their bravery and cunning in the drinking sessions that followed feasting in the chief's hall.

pitchfork used for picking up bundles of hay, it has two sharp prongs on a long pole.

terpen the Saxons built artificial hills of earth to live on in the wet lands of what is now Holland.

ornaments Saxon warriors liked fancy brooches, rings and belt buckles.

PHOTOCOPIABLE

ROMANS, ANGLO-SAXONS AND VIKINGS: The Anglo-Saxons
Why did the Anglo-Saxons come to Britain? Page 20

Flavia's story

I am Flavia, daughter of Flavius. I am 16. My father has a villa twenty miles from Londinium on the road to Durobrivae. He was a magistrate and he is now an advisor to King Vortigern. Times are very difficult but we try to live like Romans. We speak Latin in the family, though the slaves and villagers only understand Celtic. Our villa was beautiful. It had lovely mosaic floors and bright paintings on the walls. We had a good bathhouse with hot water and a hypocaust in the winter dining room. None of that works now. We have been raided twice. The first time it was the Picts, men with patterns painted on their skin from the far north. We ran away and hid in the woods while they stole our best things and set fire to our house. We managed to put the fire out after they went away, but we only have two or three rooms now which have a roof on them. We also found the bodies of five of our slaves, whom they had caught. My maid, Gwyned, was killed. I had known her all my life and I could not stop crying when we found her.

Father was called to a meeting with King Vortigern. When he came back he was angry. He said that the king had hired a barbarian Saxon called Hengest to guard us. This Saxon had about one hundred warriors and Vortigern told them they could live on the island of Tanatus. Father did not like it. He said that

Tanatus was very near our villa and he did not trust the barbarians. Father wanted to know why Vortigern's Roman soldiers could not defend us – the king said that he needed them to fight his enemies in Britain like Count Ambrosius.

Father was right! Only a year after Hengest arrived, a group of his men attacked our farm and villa. Our slaves tried to fight them but they are mostly old people and they only had their pitchforks and kitchen knives, while the Saxons were strong young men with swords and shields. We ran away again but the Saxons stole even our metal cooking pots this time and took two women slaves away with them.

Father went to King Vortigern to complain and there is to be a meeting between the Romans and the Saxons soon. Father thinks that it will end badly – every month more Saxons come to Kent. They do not stay in the island that we gave them any more. Soon Kent will be a Saxon country, then who will stop them taking more and more land? My brother is a soldier in King Vortigern's guard. He wants to fight the Saxons while we can. Father is talking about leaving Britannia altogether and sailing across the sea to Armorica. They say it is safe there. I think I agree with father. Life is too dangerous here. I want peace again.

villa a big country house usually with a farm attached.
Londinium London.
Durobrivae Rochester.
Celtic the British spoke Celtic before the Romans came, and ordinary people still used it; the Celtic language survives in Wales and Brittany today.
hypocaust a Roman central heating system that worked by leading the smoke and hot air from a fire under the floor of the room.
Picts *Picti* was the Roman name for the people who lived in north-east Scotland.
Vortigern Vortigern was a Romano-British king in southern Britain; the story of Vortigern and Hengest comes from the writing of the Welsh monk, Gildas.
Hengest Hengest was a Saxon leader who became the first Saxon king of Kent.
Tanatus the Isle of Thanet.
Ambrosius Ambrosius was another Romano-British leader who fought against Vortigern and later against the Saxons.
Armorica Brittany, a part of modern France where they still speak the Celtic language; it was called Brittany because many refugees went there from Britannia.

Name _____   Date _____

Two sides of the story

Read the two accounts.

● Why did Witta join Hengest and come to Britain?

Witta came to Britain because

● Who's fault was it that Flavia had to leave her home?

I think that it was the Saxons' fault because

I think that it was Vortigern's fault because

Place-names (1)

Prefix or suffix	Origin	Meaning	Language
Aber	Aber	mouth of the river	Gaelic
Ard	Aird	high	Gaelic
Auch	Ach	field	Gaelic
Borough	Burh, Byrig	fortified place	Old English (Saxon)
Bottom	Botm	river valley	Old English (Saxon)
Burn	Burna	stream	Old English (Saxon)
By	By	farmstead	Viking
Cader	Cadeir	seat	Celtic
Caster	Castra	Roman fort	Latin
Cester	Castra	Roman fort	Latin
Chester	Castra	Roman fort	Latin
Cliff	Clif	river bank	Old English (Saxon)
Coombe	Cumb	valley	Old English (Saxon)
Cott	Cot	cottage	Old English (Saxon)
Croft	Croft	enclosed field	Old English (Saxon)
Dale	Dael	valley	Old English (Saxon)
Den	Tun	farmstead, village	Old English (Saxon)
Don	Tun	farmstead, village	Old English (Saxon)
Eccles	Egles, Ecclesia	church	Celtic, Latin
Fold	Fald	sheepfold	Old English (Saxon)
Ford	Ford	river crossing	Old English (Saxon)
Gate	Gata	street	Viking
Gate	Geata	gap, pass	Old English (Saxon)
Ham	Ham	homestead, village	Old English (Saxon)
Hampstead	Ham stede	homestead	Old English (Saxon)
Hampton	Ham tun	home farm	Old English (Saxon)
Holt	Holt	wood	Old English (Saxon)
Hurst	Hyrst	wooded hill	Old English (Saxon)

PHOTOCOPIABLE

Place-names (2)

Prefix or suffix	Origin	Meaning	Language
Ing	Ingas	the people of	Old English (Saxon)
Inver	Inver	on the river	Gaelic
Kirk	Kirkja	church	Viking
Lan	Lann	church	Celtic
Leigh	Leah	woodland clearing, meadow	Old English (Saxon)
Llan	Llan	church	Celtic
Loch	Loch	lake	Gaelic
Mouth	Mutha	river mouth	Old English (Saxon)
Ness	Naess	headland	Viking
Pen	Penn	head, hill	Celtic
Pol	Porth	harbour	Celtic
Ross	Ros	moor	Celtic
Stowe	Stow	gathering place	Old English (Saxon)
Street	Straet	Roman road	Old English (Saxon)
Thorpe	Thorp	outlying farm	Viking
Thwaite	Thveit	meadow	Viking
Toft	Toft	house	Viking
Ton	Tun	farmstead, village	Old English (Saxon)
Tor	Torr	rocky hill	Old English (Saxon)
Vant	Fontana, Funt	fountain, spring	Latin, Old English
Wich	Wic	market	Old English (Saxon)
Wick	Wic, Vicus	place of Romano-British settlement	Old English, Latin

ROMANS, ANGLO-SAXONS AND VIKINGS: The Anglo-Saxons
What do we know about early Anglo-Saxon life? Page 23

PHOTOCOPIABLE

Plan of an Anglo-Saxon house

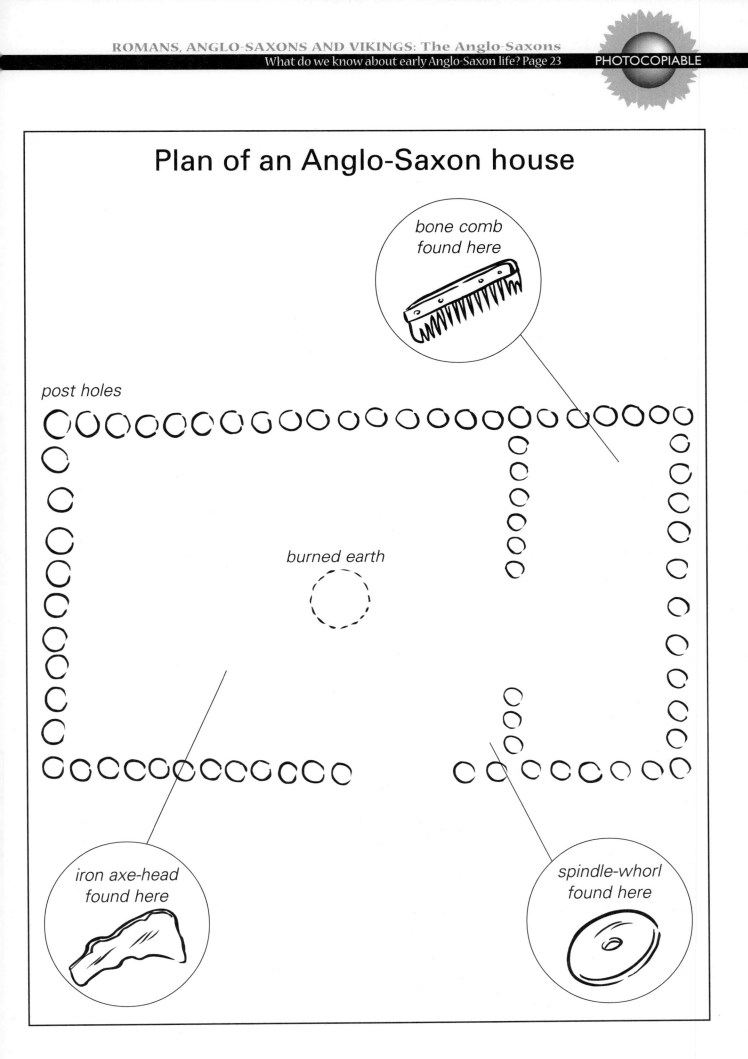

bone comb
found here

post holes

burned earth

iron axe-head
found here

spindle-whorl
found here

PHOTOCOPIABLE

ROMANS, ANGLO-SAXONS AND VIKINGS: The Anglo-Saxons
How did the Anglo-Saxons become the English? Page 24

Kingdoms in the Dark Ages

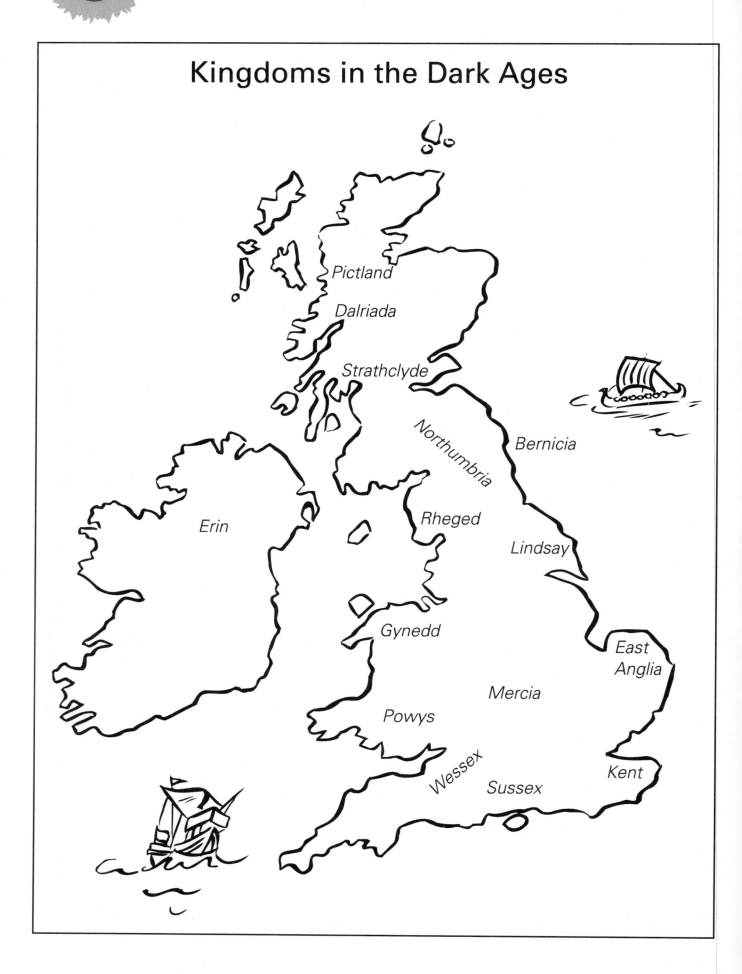

ROMANS, ANGLO-SAXONS AND VIKINGS: The Anglo-Saxons
How did the Anglo-Saxons become the English? Page 24

PHOTOCOPIABLE

The Anglo-Saxon Chronicle

This is part of *The Anglo-Saxon Chronicle*, a timeline written in Saxon times.

681 Trumbright was made Bishop of Hexham and Trumwine was made Bishop of the Picts because they were ruled by Northumbria then.

682 The Welsh attacked Northumbria, but Centwine beat them and chased them as far as the sea.

684 Egfirth sent an army to attack the Scots in Dalriada. It was led by one of his men called Briht. They burned down a lot of churches there.

685 King Egfirth ordered Cuthbert to be made a Bishop. Bishop Theodorus made him Bishop of Hexham in the cathedral at York on Easter day. King Egfirth was killed in a battle at the seaside on May 20th and lots of his men were killed too. He had been king of Northumbria for fifteen years. His brother, Aldfrith, became king next but Caedwalla, king of Wessex, began to fight him… There was bloody rain in Britain and milk and butter turned to blood.

686 Caedwalla and his brother Mul attacked Kent and the Isle of Wight…

687 Mul was burned to death in Kent with twelve other men, so Caedwalla attacked Kent again.

688 King Caedwalla went to Rome and became a Christian. He was baptised Peter. He died a week later…

697 The Mercians killed Osthryth, their own queen.

698 The Picts killed the Northumbrian lord, Brihtred.

704 Aethelred, who had been king of Mercia, became a monk.

The raid on Lindisfarne

In this year 793 there were terrible signs and omens in the Kingdom of Northumbria. We had storms with thunder and lightning that looked like fiery dragons in the sky. The crops failed and people went hungry. We thought that God was angry with us and that something awful was going to happen. On the 8th June something awful did happen!

I, Cuthbert, was in my second year as a novice at the great monastery on the holy island of Lindisfarne. My parents named me after Saint Cuthbert, who was Bishop here, and I was happy when I was old enough to start my training as a monk. I went to work in the scriptorium, where I was learning to write really well so that I could help to copy out the wonderful books in the library. I was standing beside my teacher, Brother Oswald, watching how he sketched out a beautiful letter 'I' at the beginning of a chapter, when the church bell began to ring. We knew something was wrong because it was not time for prayers. Besides, it was ringing so wildly it was as if even the bell was terrified. In the monastery we were taught to be silent and to always move about quietly with our heads down, but suddenly there were shouts and screams and running feet. Oswald looked up annoyed. "Go and see what all that noise is about." He spoke sitting on his stool, but the next minute I was looking at his body lying on the floor. A huge figure loomed over us and everything went black.

Since then my life has been a bad dream. I opened my eyes next to see the sky heaving and swaying above me, as the earth seemed to move under me. But it was not the earth, it was this ship rocking as it leaps over the moving hills of water. I was lying on my back and Brother Edwin was there, supporting my head between his knees. We were tied up and lying in the bottom of the open ship. On each side of us a row of men hauled on the long oars, backwards and forwards, heaving and grunting together. They are big men with yellow hair. They wear bright clothes and many brooches and

ROMANS, ANGLO-SAXONS AND VIKINGS: The Vikings
When did the Vikings first come to Britain? Page 30

PHOTOCOPIABLE

bracelets. Their language is strange but I can understand quite a lot of what they say. The one who brings us water tries to scare us. "Such a soft, weak boy," he says, poking me with his finger. "Who will want to buy you? I should throw you overboard or cut you up to feed the seagulls."

But they will not kill us now. I understand from their talk that many of the monks got away and they managed to save the silver cups and other valuable things from the church. Because of that they need to sell us as slaves or they will not make a profit on their raid. They talk about the attack so calmly. They have robbed God's church and slaughtered his priests, but they behave as if it was just business.

Up and down goes the ship, back and forward go the oars with a grinding and creaking of wood rubbing on wood. We are always soaking wet from rain and spray. We shiver from cold and we are very hungry. We try to say our prayers together.

The heathen men do not seem to notice the cold or wet. They laugh and joke loudly, they swear and boast and argue among themselves. Their leader stands at the stern of the ship all day with the handle of the great steering oar under his arm. He stares forward with his eyes watering from the wind. He talks gently to the ship as if it were an animal. "Forward, Wave-leaper, steady now and you will rest on the beach tomorrow."

Who are these people?

PHOTOCOPIABLE

A Viking ship

Viking ship from the top

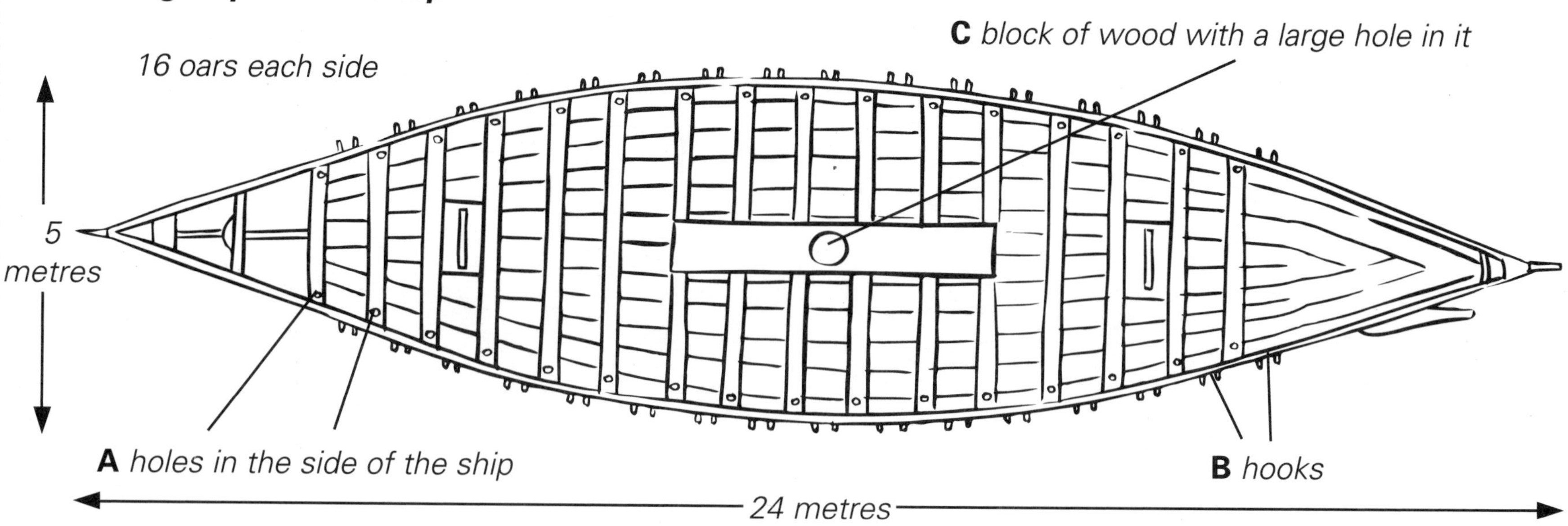

16 oars each side

5 metres

24 metres

A holes in the side of the ship

B hooks

C block of wood with a large hole in it

Artist's impression of a Viking ship

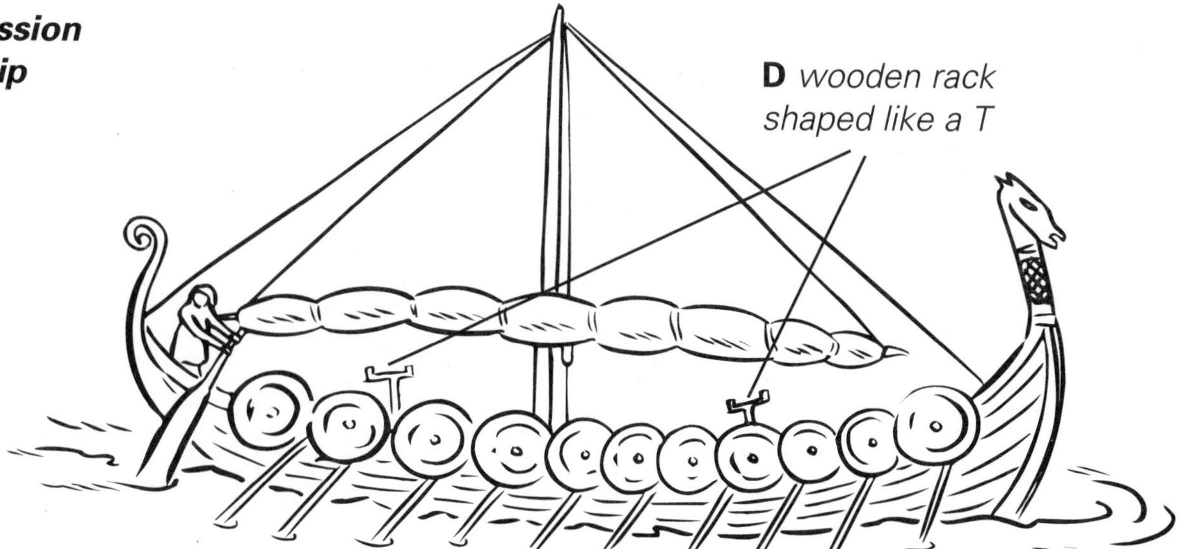

D wooden rack shaped like a T

Name _____   Date _____

A Viking ship

Look at the diagram and picture of the ship.
● What do you think the holes at A were for?

● What do you think the hooks at B were for?

● What do you think C is?

● What do you think the wooden posts at D could have been used for?

● What do you think it would have been like to sail on the Viking ship?

PHOTOCOPIABLE

A Viking burial

I heard that when a chief died they did many strange things and I was interested to learn more about it, so when I was told that an important man had died I wanted to see the funeral.

They laid him in a grave and put a roof over it for ten days, while they made new clothes for him.

Then they went to the man's slave girls and asked, "Who will die with the chief ?"

One of them answered, "I will."

Then two young women were told to look after her. They went with her everywhere, and they even washed her feet with their own hands. She was allowed to eat and drink and do what she liked.

When the day of the burning arrived, I went to the river where his ship was. I saw that they had pulled the ship onto the shore, and that they had put up four wooden posts. Beside the ship they made a big pile of wood like a tent. Then they lifted the ship up until it was on top. In the middle of the ship they made a tent and covered this with various sorts of cloth. They brought a couch and put it on the ship.

Then came an old woman that they call the Angel of Death, and she covered it with a mattress of Greek brocade. She was in charge of making the clothes and arranging everything, and she is the one who kills the girl slave. She was fat and scowling.

They put the dead man in the tent. They sat him on the mattress and propped him up with cushions. They brought beer, fruits and flowers, which they put with him, then bread, meat and onions, which they put in front of him. Then they brought a dog, which they killed and put in the ship. Then they brought his weapons and placed them by his side. Then they took two horses, ran them until they sweated, then cut them to pieces with a sword and put them in the ship. Next they killed a rooster and a hen and threw them in.

On Friday afternoon they led the slave girl to a thing that they had made which was like a door. She put her feet on the hands of the men and they lifted her up to look over the door three times. Then they brought her a hen and she cut off its head and put it in the tent. I asked the interpreter what she had done.

He answered, "The first time they raised her she said, 'I can see my father and mother.' The second time she said, 'I see all my dead relatives.' The third time she said, 'I see my master sitting in Valhalla; it is beautiful; he is calling me. Take me to him.'"

Now they took her to the ship. She took off the two bracelets she was wearing and gave them both to the old woman called the Angel of Death, who was going to kill her. Then she took off the two finger rings that she was wearing, and gave them to the two girls who had looked after her. Then the old woman made her enter the tent and she killed her and laid her beside the dead man. Then the man's relative came and took a piece of wood. He lighted it and set fire to the ship. A strong wind began to blow so that the flames flared up and burned it all.

They covered the burned ship with earth till it looked like a little hill and they wrote the man's name on a wooden post in the middle of it.

Viking place-names

Prefix or suffix	Meaning
Acr	field
Askr	ash tree
Beck	stream
Bottom	bottom of a valley
Booth	hut
By	settlement
Eik	oak tree
Garth	fenced land
Howe	mound of earth
Karl	farmer
Keld	spring of water
Kirk	church
Crook	bend in the river
Mar	marsh
Mickle	big
Moss	marsh
Mire	swamp
Ness	land sticking out into the sea
Thorpe	farm
Thwaite	meadow
Ulf	wolf

Can you find Viking place-names which contain these parts of words on your map?
Make a list of them.

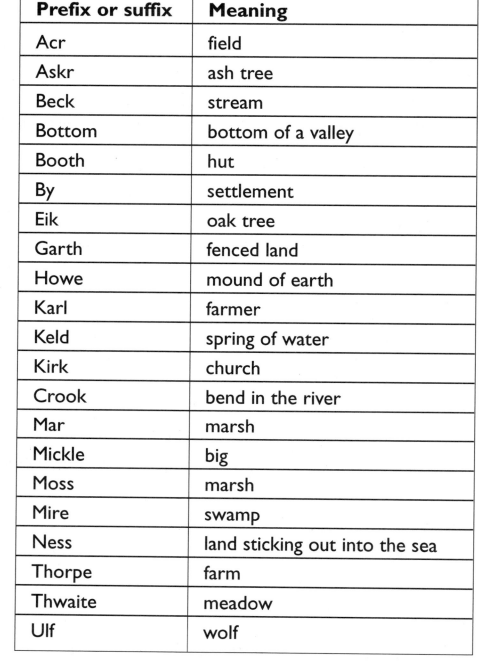

114

Name _____   Date _____

What was Henry VIII like?

● Think of three different words to describe the person in your painting. Don't forget to think about what sort of character you think he was. When you have written down the words, find the evidence for your ideas from the picture.

Words to describe Henry	Evidence in the painting

● Write a sentence describing what you think Henry was like.

We think Henry was _____

because _____

_____

● Now look at a reference book. Answer either question A or B.

A. Find out two more things about Henry.

B. Were you right about Henry? Find out two things that show that you were right or wrong about Henry.

BRITAIN AND THE WIDER WORLD IN TUDOR TIMES: Henry VIII
What was the Northern Renaissance? Page 41

PHOTOCOPIABLE

Name _____   Date _____

Characteristics of a Renaissance man or woman

Tick the boxes if you think the statement applies to a cultured person.

☐ *Was able to read and write fluently.*

☐ *Was able to speak more than one language.*

☐ *Had been born twice.*

☐ *Wore fashionable clothes.*

☐ *Liked funny jokes.*

☐ *Knew about some of the ideas from Ancient Greece and Rome.*

☐ *Was athletic and keen on dancing.*

☐ *Didn't want to know about new ideas.*

☐ *Only believed what the Pope in Rome told them.*

☐ *Was able to compose music or paint pictures that looked realistic.*

Read the description of Henry VIII. Do you think that Henry VIII was a Renaissance prince or not?

Give two reasons to explain your answer.

● _____

● _____

England meets France

Kit Montague stood on a rolling hillside, looking across the valley at the French company drawn up on the opposing hill. The sun shone on the shining armour and rich clothing of the assembled host. King Henry looked especially splendid in his scarlet and gold brocade, and mounted on a spirited white charger. He was tall and athletic, every inch a royal prince. Kit felt his heart swell with pride as he looked across at his monarch. The brassy squall of trumpets and sackbuts rang out and the massed courts began to advance down the Val d'Or towards each other. There was a ripple of tension throughout the ranks.

"Would the advance become a charge?" wondered Kit nervously.

Slowly the two kings approached each other. They leaned forward and gave each other the formal embrace of kingship. A great cheer rang out across the valley. The kings dismounted and embraced again. Kit was proud to see that Henry's head rose above that of the French king. Henry led them all in procession towards a huge building in the centre of the valley. As they drew closer Kit realised with surprise that it was in fact a gigantic tent. He marvelled at the workmanship that had constructed it. It was no more impressive, however, than the tents of cloth of gold that their own king had brought. They had been erected on the hillside above them and dazzled everyone in the sun.

In front of the pavilion where the king and queen were to lodge stood an ornate fountain. It seemed to be surrounded by a throng of poorly dressed peasants who were pushing forward to drink. "The ale cannot be so bad that one has to drink water," remarked Joscylin Duberry, one of Kit's fellow squires.

BRITAIN AND THE WIDER WORLD IN TUDOR TIMES: Henry VIII

PHOTOCOPIABLE   *What was important about* The Field of the Cloth of Gold? Page 43

They laughed at the horror on his face at this sad prospect, but suddenly realised the fountain flowed with wine, not water. "What an amazing extravagance," murmured Joscylin admiringly. In the distance they could see the main tilting yard where the jousts would take place. As they neared the tourney field they could hear the creak of wood and leather and the clang of metal as the French knights practised for the tournament the next day. "They will need all the practice they can get," Kit observed to Joscylin. "We have the cream of English knights with us and will prove our prowess in the feats of arms tomorrow."

All around were rich, mouth-watering smells as the cooks prepared the welcome banquet. From a huge beehive oven, steaming loaves of finest white bread were being carried to the cooks' tents to join the whole hogs and oxen roasting over roaring fires. Everywhere Kit looked there were signs of industry. Hundreds of servants of both countries scurried, like busy worker ants, backwards and forwards on their lords' business. Food and drink, rich clothing, burnished mail and people – all were on the move across the valley from one tent to another.

Kit looked forward to the evening's festivities. While Joscylin and he would be serving at the high table there was also a chance to watch the entertainment, such as the extravagant firework display that would take place that night.

The king dismounted to enter the pavilion. Kit's heart swelled with pride as he looked at him; surely there was no finer prince in all Christendom! He was young and handsome. He glittered gold and scarlet from the top of his splendid red-gold hair to his square-toed, burnished-gold slippers. Henry's loud, exuberant royal laugh rang out over the assembled company as he flung back his head, delighting in all he saw, while Kit marvelled at the vast display of wealth so lavishly displayed all around.

BRITAIN AND THE WIDER WORLD IN TUDOR TIMES: Henry VIII
What happened between Henry and Anne? Page 45

PHOTOCOPIABLE

Name _____   Date _____

Henry's 'Great Matter'

What is the name of the character that you are finding out about?

I am finding out about _____

Write down three things that you have found out about your character:

●

●

●

What did you use to find out about your character?

Make a list of any books, CD-ROMs or websites that you used.

Draw the head and shoulders of your character. Use a speech bubble to explain how your character feels about the divorce.

Why do you think your character feels this way?

I think my character feels _____

because _____

PHOTOCOPIABLE

BRITAIN AND THE WIDER WORLD IN TUDOR TIMES: Henry VIII
Why did Thomas More have to die? Page 48

Name _____   Date _____

Why did Thomas More have to die?

Spokesperson
You will have to report the conclusions that your group comes to.

Scribe
You will have to write down your group's ideas.

● Which group do you belong to? Circle the group.

Group A – Henry VIII   Group B – Thomas More

Henry has asked Thomas More to take an oath that will recognise that Henry is in charge of the Church of England. This will mean that Henry will no longer allow the Pope in Rome to tell him what to do. Thomas More is not prepared to take this oath.

● Think about the point of view of your character. Why might your character want to behave in a certain way? Think about two or three things that you would say.

Group A
What reasons could Henry have for wanting Thomas to take the oath?

We think Thomas should take the oath because _____

_____

Group B
Why would Thomas not be prepared to take the oath?

We do not think Thomas should have to take the oath because _____

_____

BRITAIN AND THE WIDER WORLD IN TUDOR TIMES: Henry VIII
Why was the *Mary Rose* important? Page 50

PHOTOCOPIABLE

The *Mary Rose*

Your group has a number of pieces of information to discover. Work together to find all the different elements and use the sources you have been given. Record all of your findings on a large poster and illustrate it, if you have time.

● Find a picture of a Tudor warship. Copy the picture and label the different parts.

● Explain how the warship moved and how people at this time navigated.

● On your map of the British Isles and Northern Europe, mark in the following locations:

| Brest | St Malo | Boulogne | Calais | Edinburgh |
| Antwerp | Paris | London | Plymouth | Portsmouth |

● Make a timeline showing what happened to the *Mary Rose*.

● Describe three or four things about the life of a Tudor sailor.

● Explain why the *Mary Rose* was important.

The royal visit

Young Bet Harrington woke to the sound of hammering and clattering, the sound of chests being dragged across wooden floors and horses neighing and stamping in the courtyard. "She has arrived," she thought and jumped out of bed to look out of the window. But it was not the queen on a white palfrey, just another wagon full of boxes and bundles being unloaded under the supervision of a bossy court usher.

Months ago, a court officer had ridden up to ask if anyone in the village had had the plague recently, then he had looked at the house and the views from the windows. At last he had announced that her father, Sir William, should prepare to receive Her Majesty the Queen for one night some time in June. Ever since then there had been no peace or rest for anyone.

Her father had gone to London immediately to borrow money and to discuss the matter with friends at court. Soon builders were at work preparing the chamber in which the queen would sleep. The old stone walls of the manor house were covered with new wooden panelling, and a big new window made of little diamonds of glass was cut into the wall so that the queen could look out across the gardens.

"But it is only for one night," said Bet's mother.

"It is a great honour," replied her father. "Other people have their houses rebuilt when they are expecting a visit from her. Anyway, I have wanted to modernise that room for a long time."

Bet remembered how a month ago, the yeoman purveyor and his men had come and ordered the food and the firewood and the hay for the horses. Cartloads had started arriving from all the local farms and the yard had often been full of farmers arguing about prices.

BRITAIN AND THE WIDER WORLD IN TUDOR TIMES: The Elizabethan age

How did Queen Elizabeth meet her people? Page 55   PHOTOCOPIABLE

With six days to wait until the special day, the gentleman usher had come with ten men to prepare the house. Bet's family had had to move into the servants' rooms as the queen's furniture was being moved in and new locks were being put on the doors. Tapestries had been hung up and the queen's silver plates had been unpacked. Tents had been erected in the park for all the hundreds of retainers who could not find room in the houses around.

Two days ago, the wardrobe officer had come. Bet had crept into her old room to see the queen's beautiful dresses and jewellery laid out, with rustling silks and satins and glittering golden thread and diamond studs.

Now Bet watched as the queen came from the gatehouse. Over the hill came the first horsemen, then following came an endless procession of brightly coloured figures. The sun flashed from the halberds and poleaxes of the guards, the breeze shook out the banners. Then the queen was in sight and a cheer came from the crowd of villagers waiting by the lane. They took off their hats and bowed and curtsied as she passed by. Bet saw Simon Noakes, the schoolmaster, step forward to make the speech of welcome that he had been preparing for weeks. She saw Her Majesty stop her horse to listen. Master Noakes looked terrified but she was smiling at him and answering. Then she came on to the gate.

Her face was white and her hair red and curly. She wore a lace ruff around her neck and a green velvet riding-gown studded with pearls. Her farthingale spread the dress gracefully over the beautiful white horse. Bet's father looked nervous as he went down on one knee. "Welcome to Benhope Manor, Your Majesty," was all he managed to say. Bet was leaning forward from the gatehouse window now, looking straight down on the queen. Then it happened. Bet's moppet slipped out of her hand and fell right into the queen's lap. Her Majesty looked up…

BRITAIN AND THE WIDER WORLD IN TUDOR TIMES: The Elizabethan age

PHOTOCOPIABLE *What was the Elizabethan countryside like? Page 57*

Verses from Thomas Tusser

October
Where water all winter, annoieth too much,
bestow not thy wheat upon land that is such:
But rather sow oates, or else bullimong there,
gray peason or runcials, fitches or tare.

✳

November
Foul privies are now, to be cleansed and side,
let night be appointed, such baggage to hide:
Which buried in garden, in trenches allow,
shall make very many things, better to grow.

✳

January
Thy garden plot lately, wel trenched and mucked,
would now be twifallowed, the mallowes plucked out:
Wel clensed and purged, of root and of stone,
that fault therein afterward, found may be none.

✳

March
In March and in April, from morning til night,
in sowing and setting, good housewifes delight:
To have in a garden, or other such plot,
to trim up their house and to furnish their pot.

> **Bullimong, runcials** and **fitches** different sorts of grain.
> **peason** peas.
> **Privies** toilets – they were emptied to make manure for the garden.
> **Twifallowed** dug twice.
> **Setting** planting.

Map of Elizabethan London

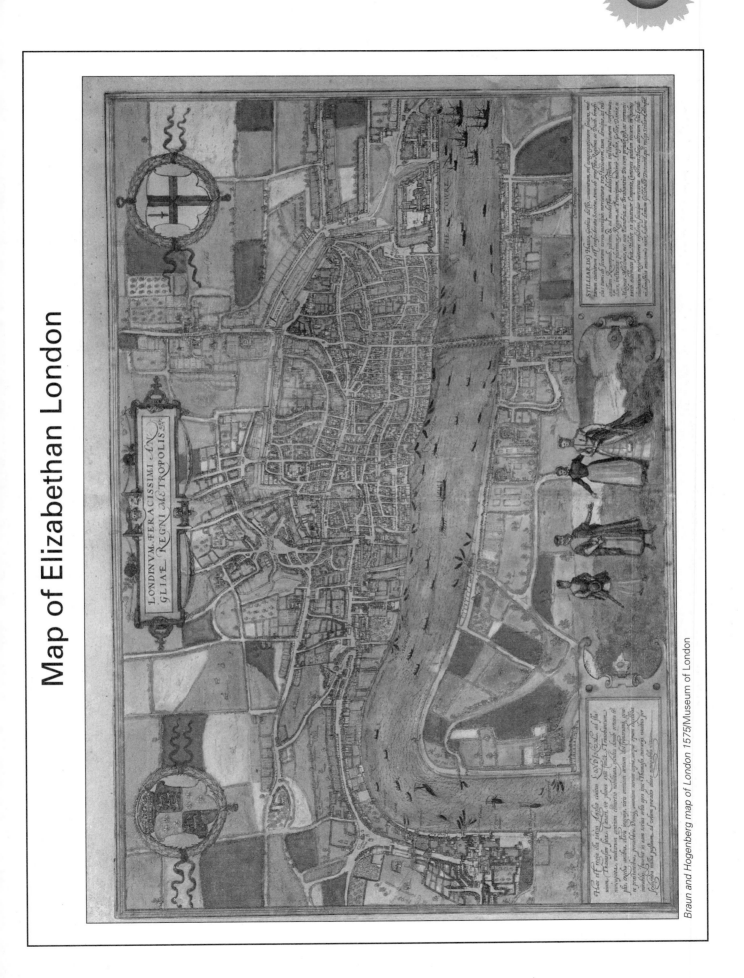

Braun and Hogenberg map of London 1575/Museum of London

Shakespeare's life

1564 William Shakespeare was born at Stratford-upon-Avon. His father was Richard Shakespeare, he was a **whittawer** which means he made gloves and other things from leather. Shakespeare was baptised on 25 April and many people think that his birthday was 23 April, but we cannot be sure of this. He probably went to Stratford Grammar School (now King Edward VI). Schoolboys in those days started by learning the alphabet from a **hornbook** (a piece of board with the letters on it covered with a thin sheet of cow's horn). Later they learned to read the Latin language. Shakespeare probably read *Aesop's Fables* in Latin. One of Shakespeare's friends later said that he could read some Latin and a bit of Greek. When he left school he probably went to work for his father.

1582 When he was 18, he married a woman called Anne Hathaway.

1585 William and Anne had twins – they were called Hamnet and Judith.

1587 When he was 23 he went off, leaving his wife behind. Some people say that he had to run away because he had been **poaching** (killing deer on a rich man's land). Other people think that he might have worked for a while as a private teacher for a rich man's children. He ended up in London working in the theatres. He was probably an actor before he began to write plays.

1593 The London theatres were closed because of the **plague**. From December 1592 until December 1593, 10 675 people died of the plague. Shakespeare published his first poem and he published two more in the next few years. He wrote the poems for rich men, who probably helped him by giving him money.

1594 –1599 Shakespeare wrote lots of his most famous plays. He was still acting in them himself as well as being one of the managers of his theatre company.

1599 The Globe theatre was built and Shakespeare owned a share of it.

1603 Queen Elizabeth died and King James took the throne. Shakespeare and his men acted many plays for the king.

1611 Shakespeare retired and went home to Stratford to live in a house that he had built for his family. His twin children both died young but his youngest daughter was there to look after him. Her name was Susanna and she married a doctor.

1616 Shakespeare died. He was buried in the church in Stratford and the words on his grave say:

> Good frend for Jesus sake forbeare,
> To digg the dust enclosed heare.
> Bleste be ye man yt spares thes stones,
> And curst be he yt moves my bones.

Shakespeare

Portrait of William Shakespeare (1564–1616), engraving by English School (19th century)
Private Collection/Ken Welsh/Bridgeman Art Library

Portrait of Shakespeare from Mr William's Shakespeare's Comedies, Histories and Tragedies
British Library, London, UK/Bridgeman Art Library

BRITAIN AND THE WIDER WORLD IN TUDOR TIMES: The Elizabethan age
Who was William Shakespeare? Page 61

PHOTOCOPIABLE

The Globe theatre

London Globe Theatre 1596/AKG (London)

The Spanish Armada

Background

1554 Queen Mary Tudor married King Philip II of Spain. He wanted to become king of England but most English people did not want him because he was Spanish and a Roman Catholic.

1558 Mary died and Elizabeth became queen. Philip still wanted to be king of England and he tried to marry Elizabeth, but she refused. Elizabeth was a Protestant and many Roman Catholic people wanted her cousin, Mary Queen of Scots, to be queen instead because she was a Catholic. English sailors like Francis Drake attacked Spanish ships and Spanish towns in the Americas to steal the silver the Spanish mined there. Elizabeth would not punish them and sometimes she took some of the treasure herself.

1586 Mary Stuart, Queen of Scots, nominated Philip II as her successor to the English throne.

1587 In February Mary Queen of Scots was executed for trying to kill Elizabeth. Philip decided to invade England and make himself king. In April Sir Francis Drake sailed to Spain and raided the ports, attacking and burning the Armada ships while they were at anchor. This slowed down the preparations for the invasion.

The Armada Year, 1588

28–30 May
The Spanish Armada set sail. It took a long time to get to England because it stopped to take on supplies and the weather was bad on the way.

29 July
The Armada was first spotted near Cornwall. The English fleet set out from Plymouth to meet it.

31 July
The battle near Plymouth. The Spanish lost two ships.

1–4 August
The English fleet followed the Armada east, fighting near Weymouth, Portland Bill and off the Isle of Wight.

5 and 6 August
The Armada sailed towards France to try to pick up the Spanish army to bring them across the Channel. They anchored near Calais but failed to meet the army.

7 August
The English set fire to some of their own ships and floated them into the Armada to try to burn it. The Spanish scattered to get out of the way of the fireships.

8 August
The Battle of Gravelines where there was fierce fighting. It was difficult for the Spanish because there was a strong wind blowing them towards sandbanks and away from the English they were trying to attack. Both sides ran out of ammunition. That afternoon the wind changed and the Spanish ships were blown away from the coast and towards the North Sea.

10–12 August
The Spanish decided to give up and try to get home by sailing right around Britain and Ireland to get back to Spain. The English chased them North.

12 August
The English went back home for supplies.

Late August and September
The Armada sailed through terrible storms that split them up and wrecked many ships off Scotland and Ireland.

BRITAIN AND THE WIDER WORLD IN TUDOR TIMES: The Elizabethan age

PHOTOCOPIABLE   How was the Armada destroyed? Page 62

Letters to Count Philip Fugger

Hamburg 23rd June 1588

I simply must tell you that the skipper, Hans Limburger, has arrived here with his ship from Cadiz. He got through with a cargo of salt, wine, raisins, cinnamon and some sugar. He set off on 20th May. In the distance he saw the Spanish Armada and sailed beside it all day. The next day the wind was strong and he could not see it any more but he thought it was heading for the English Channel.

Further on he met an English warship and they made him sail to Plymouth with them. Captain Drake entertained him for three days. Apparently the English were happy that the Spanish were coming at last. Afterwards Captain Drake gave Limburger a pass to let him through the English fleet. Then the English put to sea in spite of the bad wind.

If there is a fight a lot of men will be killed. For two days the sun and moon have looked red as blood. God only knows what that means!

Middleburg 22nd July 1588

The English mail has come in bringing letters. In one it says that a boat arrived from Lisbon saying that it had met two lots of ships from the Spanish Armada. The first time it was twelve and the second time seventeen, all of them were badly damaged. When they asked what had happened to the rest of the Armada the Spaniards said that they did not know because they had all split up in a storm.

Drake and Admiral Lord Howard are still at sea and we do not know what has happened to them. We should hear soon as the wind is coming from England now. Some people think Drake might have been lost in the storm.

Hamburg 5th August 1588

It is reported that the English fleet has beaten the Spanish Armada. They captured twenty-two ships and sunk eighteen. Many ships were burned. Two hundred Spanish officers have been taken prisoner to England... The English are chasing what is left of the Armada... Now the English will be free to steal and attack our ships even more. God help us!

Prague 30th August 1588

Yesterday a messenger came from Milan with the announcement that the Spanish Armada has fought the English and the English have been beaten. Everyone here is celebrating, but we do not know if it is true yet.

WORLD HISTORY: Ancient Egypt

What did Howard Carter find? Page 68   PHOTOCOPIABLE

• • • • • • • • • • • • • • PRESS RELEASE • • • • • • • • • • • •

Magnificent discovery in the Valley of the Kings

On Sunday 5th November 1922, I discovered a stone door at the bottom of a set of twelve steps. The steps had been concealed by a variety of rubble and it took almost the whole of the day to clear enough to see what we had found. Towards sunset on the Sunday we had uncovered enough so that I could see part of a plastered doorway. Most excitingly the seals on the door appeared intact. The seal impressions suggested it belonged to someone of high standing as they showed that of the well-known Royal Necropolis but I was unable to discover any more at that time. I immediately sent a cable to Lord Carnarvon to let him know about my find and to encourage him to join me at once.

On 23rd November 1922, Lord Carnarvon arrived and was present when we discovered the name of the occupant of the tomb. The seal impressions were those of Tut.ankh.Amen and the Royal Necropolis. We discovered a passage of some nine metres long with another sealed door at the end.

On Sunday 26th November 1922, while Lord Carnarvon, Lady Evelyn Herbert and Arthur 'Pecky' Callender looked on, I breached a tiny hole in the door and inserted an iron testing rod to see if there was a space beyond the door. Holding a candle up to test the air I peered in. In the candle's flickering light I could see a medley of strange and beautiful things. When Lord Carnarvon enquired if I could see anything I replied, 'Yes, wonderful things!' We were all overcome by the wealth and variety of the artefacts within the chamber.

On Monday 27th November 1922, now accompanied by Ibrahim Effendi from the Egyptian Department of Antiquities, we stepped for the first time into the antechamber of the tomb. We found evidence that ancient tomb robbers had been before us but they had obviously been caught and the tomb had been resealed in antiquity. We all felt humble as we looked at the evidence of the past, the bowl half full of mortar left by the door, a finger mark on what was then new paint and a small farewell wreath dropped in the doorway. It seemed as if the room had only just been left.

On 29th November 1922, the tomb was officially opened and then resealed against thieves. After carefully photographing the artefacts in situ and then conserving the more fragile pieces, the first objects were removed from the tomb on Christmas Day 1922.

There is a burial chamber that we hope conceals the mummy of King Tut.ankh.Amen. Once the contents of the antechamber and annexe have been catalogued and safely stored the burial chamber will be investigated.

• •

WORLD HISTORY: Ancient Egypt
What did Howard Carter find? Page 68

PHOTOCOPIABLE

Name _____   Date _____

What did Howard Carter find?

● What is the name of the character?

_____

● What sort of job did he do and what does this involve?

_____

_____

● Where had he been searching and for how long had he been searching?

_____

_____

● What did he discover?

_____

● What did he do about his discovery?

_____

_____

● Why might this discovery be important?

_____

_____

● How do you think the character feels about his discovery and why do you think this?

_____

_____

_____

Name _____   Date _____

Treasures in the tomb

Look at pictures of the artefacts found in the tomb. Choose three to investigate more closely. Use reference materials to help you find answers to the questions below.

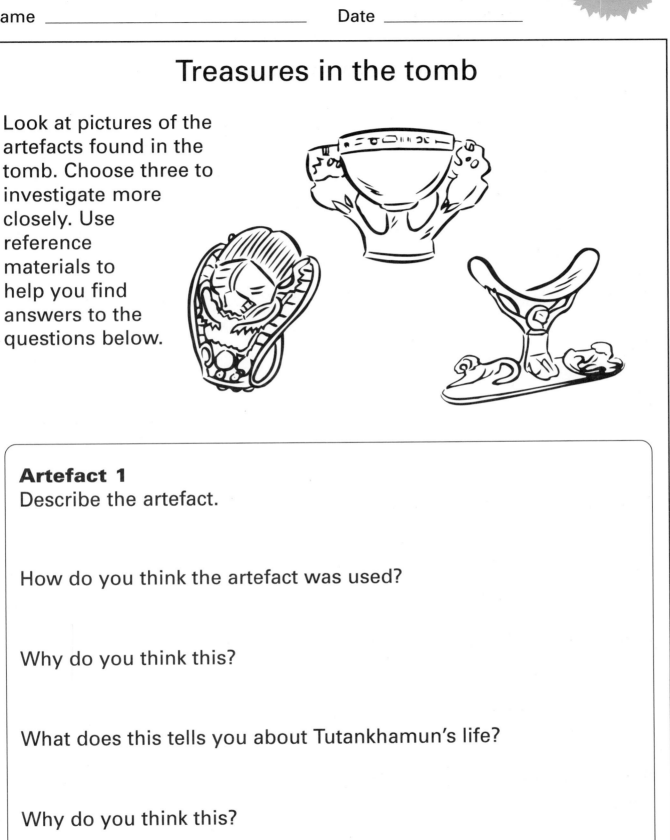

Artefact 1
Describe the artefact.

How do you think the artefact was used?

Why do you think this?

What does this tells you about Tutankhamun's life?

Why do you think this?

Name _____   Date _____

Artefact 2
Describe the artefact.

How do you think the artefact was used?

Why do you think this?

What does this tells you about Tutankhamun's life?

Why do you think this?

Artefact 3
Describe the artefact.

How do you think the artefact was used?

Why do you think this?

What does this tells you about Tutankhamun's life?

Why do you think this?

WORLD HISTORY: Ancient Egypt
How was Akhenaten different? Page 71

PHOTOCOPIABLE

Nefer-tari, the sculptor's daughter

Nefer-tari hurried across the courtyard of her parents' home towards her father's workshop. Tuthmosis was one of the craftsmen and artists who had moved to the new city of Akhetaten following the brilliant young pharaoh Akhenaten. Her father knew more about the pharaoh and his beautiful wife than most. He was one of the official sculptors and was working on a statue of the king and on two busts of Nefertiti. The queen was stunningly lovely and Nefer-tari was certain that her father's work was going to be a triumph. The queen was bound to be pleased as it showed her as beautiful as she was in real life.

Nefer-tari thought about some of the strange ideas of the new pharaoh. He felt that truth in all things was important including art. He wanted people to be shown as they really were and not as some perfect image. Nefer-tari thought that if she looked like the pharaoh she would not want people to be too truthful. He was stoop-shouldered and fat-bellied with a long head and strange, charismatic, almond-shaped eyes.

Nefer-tari liked the idea of showing the surrounding land as realistically as possible. Her mother had arranged to have scenes of the river painted on the walls of their home. Nefer-tari loved to look at the birds and water plants. The papyrus seemed to be blowing in a gentle breeze and it seemed at times as if the fish might swim off the walls.

Akhenaten had other strange ideas. He liked to be surrounded by his family. He and Nefertiti could be seen driving through the city in a gold and silver chariot while his daughters laughed and urged the horses on. Akhenaten loved his little girls and often kissed and cuddled them in public. "It was very strange," thought Nefer-tari. "Surely that is not how a pharaoh behaves?"

However, Akhenaten's strangest ideas were to do with religion. Nefer-tari was not sure she understood why it was no longer right to worship the old gods. The pharaoh said that there was only Aten, the sun god, and that all should worship as he and the queen did, at the great temple that he had built in the city. Certainly the temple was beautiful, so open and light, not like the other dark, secret temples of the old gods. But how would the ordinary person now travel to the afterlife with no gods to guide them? Nefer-tari missed the little household shrine that they had had before to Ptah, the god of craftsmen. "Sometimes," thought Nefer-tari, "changes are hard to understand."

Nefer-tari slipped into the workshop and sat quietly in the corner, as silent as a little brown mouse, watching while her father chipped away at the limestone head of Queen Nefertiti. The workshop was full of the bright white light of the Egyptian sun. Aten was surely smiling on Tuthmosis and his work! Not far away Nefer-tari could hear the sound of the Nile, the life blood of Eygpt, flowing south to the old capital of Thebes and north to the pyramids at Giza. The walls of the workshop were plain with none of the painted scenes that were found in the people's houses. Along the mud-brick walls stood shelves with caskets containing some of the tools of Tuthmosis's trade – copper saws and chisels, cakes of different pigments, palettes and reed brushes. Small boxes held the minerals used for making paints and the precious metals and stones such as Afgan turquoise to use as an inlay for emphasis and to show wealth. Soon Tuthmosis would begin to paint the plain bust and add the details that would make the statue come alive as he had with the first he had made. From a high shelf the face of the beautiful queen gazed down enigmatically at little Nefer-tari, keeping all its secrets to itself as it had and always would.

Akhenaten, pharaoh of Egypt

● Draw a diagram to show where Akhenaten came in the line of pharaohs.

● Who was pharaoh before him?

● Who were the two pharaohs who came after him?

● Can you find any connections between these people?

● Who was Akhenaten married to and what can you find out about her?

● Find out two things about Akhenaten's daughters.

● What do you think of Akhenaten's relationship with his family and why do you think this?

● Using reference, draw a picture of two of the people you have investigated.

● Write a paragraph describing what Akhenaten looked like.

● Look at some of the things that Akhenaten did and then try to explain why Akhenaten was not a typical pharaoh.

WORLD HISTORY: Ancient Egypt
How was Akhenaten different? Page 71

PHOTOCOPIABLE

The worship of Aten

● Draw images to show how Amun-Re and Aten were portrayed.

● What differences do you notice about how they were portrayed?

● Why did Akhenaten think Aten was so important?

● How did Akhenaten go about changing the religion of Egypt from the worship of many gods to that of just Aten? Explain two of the things he did.

● Try to find out how the worship of Aten was different from that of the other gods (look at the type of temple Akhenaten built).

● How did Akhenaten show that he was a follower of Aten (think of his name)? Did something similar happen to anyone else?

● Explain why you think the priests of Amun-Re were angry with Akhenaten's ideas.

● Copy out part of Akhenaten's poem, *Great Hymn to Aten*.

● Decorate your copy of the poem with pictures of animals and plants. Use the reference material to find some pictures to copy. Remember to make your pictures of animals and plants realistic.

138

139

Ancient Egyptian pyramids

● Find and draw a picture of the oldest type of pyramid.

● Where was it built and what was the name of the architect?

● How did this pyramid differ from those built later at Giza?

● Describe the pyramids on the Giza plateau.

● Find three words that can be used to describe particular features of pyramids or pyramid building.

● Why was the pyramid built?

● Explain how you think the pyramid may have been built.

The pyramids at Giza

● Find out at least four facts about one of the pyramids at Giza.

● Describe the Sphinx.

● What was the purpose of the Sphinx?

● Give three ideas about what you think it would have been like to have been one of the workers on the pyramid site.

● Would you have preferred to be a general workman or a stonemason and why do you think this?

● Find four words that can be used to describe particular features of pyramids or pyramid building.

● Why do you think the pharaohs built the pyramids?

WORLD HISTORY: Ancient Egypt
What were the pyramids for? Page 73

PHOTOCOPIABLE

Pharaohs and their pyramids

● Describe the site of the pyramids at Giza.

● Explain why you think some of the other buildings were built.

● Find out what the following structures were used for:
mortuary chapel, Queen's pyramids, the causeway, valley temple.

● Describe what you think it would have been like to have been one of the people who worked at the complex.

● What difficulties might you encounter when building pyramids?

● Find five words that can be used to describe particular features of the complex at Giza.

● Give two reasons why you think the pyramids were built.

● Why do you think the pyramid was important for:
a) the pharaoh, b) one of the ordinary people?

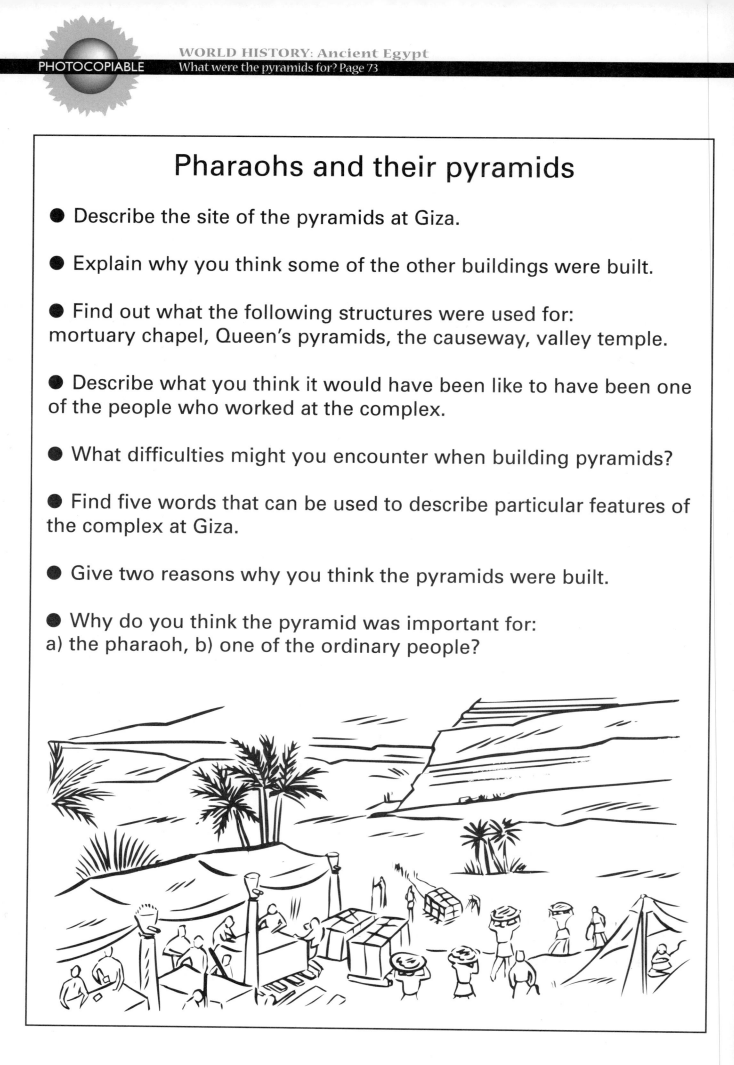

Imhotep and the water garden

Esa carried the tray of breakfast food from the kitchen through to the women's quarters where her mistress, Kawit, and her two young children, Imhotep and Teti, would be waiting for her. The beer was cool and the fruit was juicy and fresh. The bread had been baked that morning and was still warm. Esa knew that the children would be hungry and eager to break their fast. As Esa entered, Kawit was just plaiting Teti's scalp lock and tying in a fish amulet to protect her against crocodiles. The family lived near the river and Kawit was always afraid that one of the children would wander too close to the river banks where the monstrous beasts lived. The great River Nile with its busy quays and bustling warehouses was part of the family's life. Yahmose, the children's father, was one of the officials responsible for collecting, sorting and storing the vast quantity of goods that arrived each day for the pharaoh and his palace.

Kawit had a number of jobs for Esa to do that morning. The most important was a visit to the market to buy provisions for the next couple of days. Esa listened carefully to ensure that she remembered everything that her mistress wanted. Her heart sank when she heard that Kawit wanted her to take Imhotep with her. Teti was usually quiet and well behaved, except when with her brother. Imhotep was curious and fearless and full of mischief. It was no surprise that he was always in trouble.

"You must take our offering to the Great Temple before you go to the market," ordered Kawit, pulling out two full baskets made of plaited papyrus. "Imhotep will help you carry them and act as our representative," she added.

Esa saw that Imhotep was wearing his best kilt of the finest pleated linen with his eyes freshly decorated with kohl. He also had on his most innocent expression. Esa knew that look. It usually meant trouble!

Esa and Imhotep set off early to walk to the temple while the day was still cool. As they trudged through the garden Esa could see Kawit and Teti already settled by the side of the ornamental pond in the shade of the trees. The fig trees and acacia were covered with sweet-smelling blossom and Esa wished that she could have been the one watching the lotus flowers opening to the sun as Teti played at the water's edge.

WORLD HISTORY: Ancient Egypt
What was life like in the city? Page 77

PHOTOCOPIABLE

Esa and Imhotep walked along the wide, royal road towards the Great Temple. Imhotep kept wanting to scuff his sandals through the stone drainage channel in the middle of the dusty road but Esa persuaded him to keep himself relatively tidy. They passed the busy market with stalls full of fresh fruit and vegetables piled high in colourful and fragrant heaps. There were succulent purple figs, rosy pomegranates, juicy green melons, sweet shrivelled dates and clusters of grapes. Another stall had geese and ducks hanging in rows, their soft feathers dull now in death. Esa's favourite was the fish stall where the fish, large and small, glistened in the hot sunlight. Kawit had also given Esa instructions to bring back a new, decorated pot to hold her lotus flowers and papyrus-reed decoration. Somehow the old one had been broken. Esa felt she knew who might have been involved! She had seen a beautiful cream and turquoise vase that she thought would be suitable but she needed to look more carefully before she bought it. Her mistress had given her some silver and she wanted to spend it wisely.

The baskets were growing heavy and Esa was keen to leave them and visit the market, so the two headed swiftly to the offering tables in the sunlit courtyard of the temple. Imhotep made his bow to the shaven-headed priests in their leopard skins and presented his family's gift to the great god Aten.

Free from their heavy burden, the two set off thankfully for the market once more. Esa was already thinking of the wares on offer at the potter's stall. They hurried passed the vast storehouses towards the splendid King's Hall with its tall, brightly painted, stone pillars. As they passed the King's Hall there was a terrible commotion. One of the sacred cats rushed out chasing a tiny monkey that screeched as it leapt for safety up the decorated pillars towards the roof. Before Esa could stop him Imhotep had joined all the others rushing after the frightened animal. He ran swiftly across the bridge over the royal road towards the palace itself. Esa trailed miserably after him. She had known that Imhotep would get into trouble! A flash of white linen kilt showed Imhotep vanishing into the gardens still pursuing the frightened monkey. Esa ran along a bright corridor covered with pictures of fish and water plants. Suddenly she emerged into brilliant sunlight. In front of her was a beautiful garden with a small artificial lake surrounded with trees, papyrus and slender lotus flowers. Up to his knees in water, with his best kilt irretrievably ruined, stood Imhotep, triumphantly holding the screaming monkey by its long tail!

The city of Akhetaten

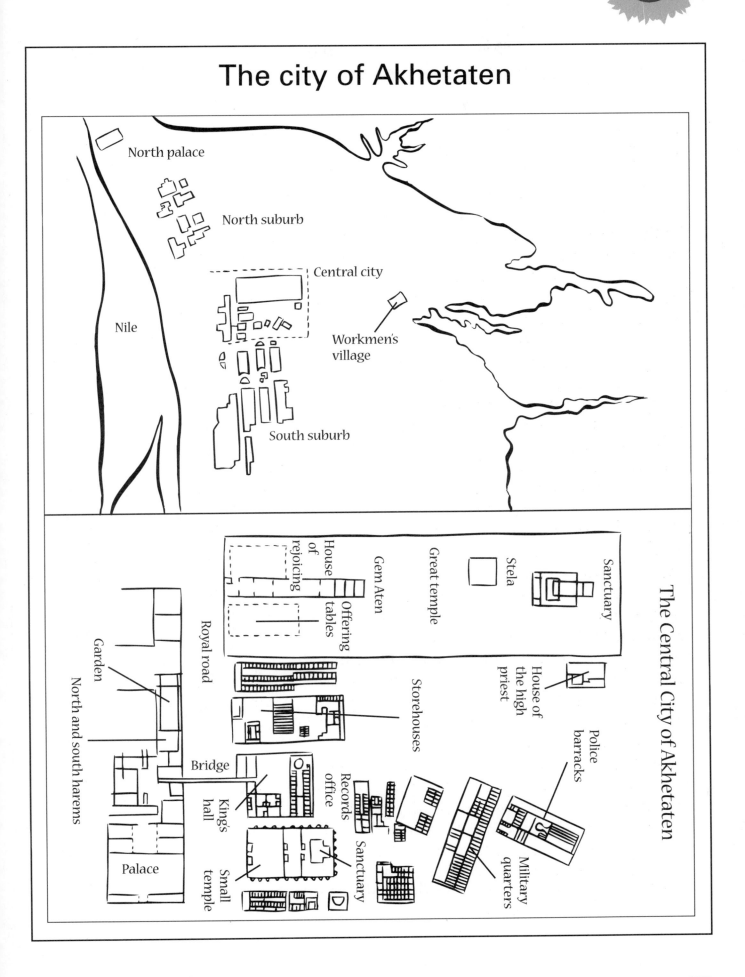

The Central City of Akhetaten

PHOTOCOPIABLE

WORLD HISTORY: Ancient Egypt
What was life like in the city? Page 77

An official's house in Akhetaten

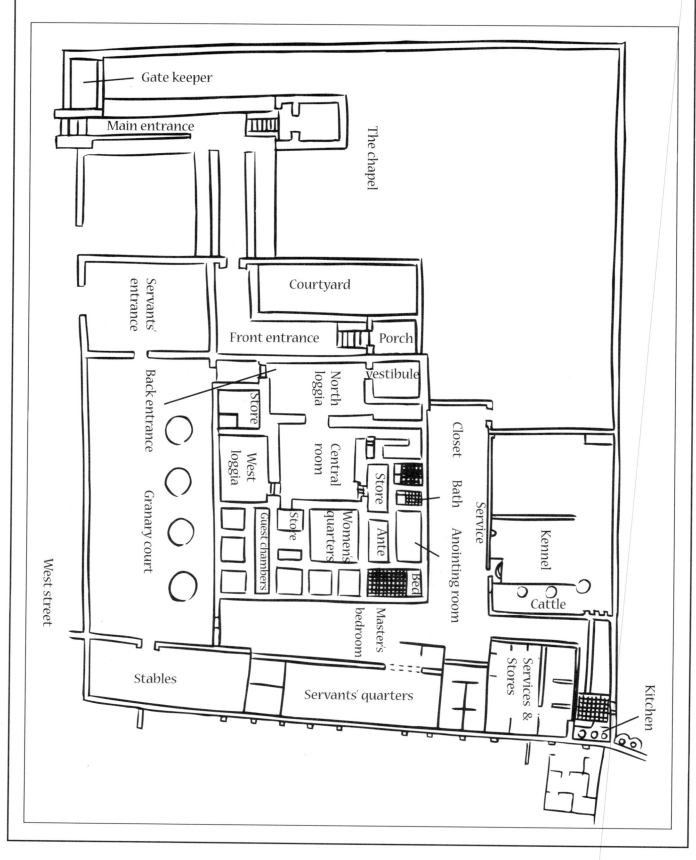

Gate keeper

Main entrance

The chapel

Servants' entrance

Courtyard

Front entrance

Porch

Back entrance

Vestibule

Store

North loggia

West loggia

Central room

Closet

Bath

Service

Store

Women's quarters

Ante

Anointing room

Kennel

Granary court

Guest chambers

Store

Bed

Cattle

West street

Master's bedroom

Services & Stores

Kitchen

Stables

Servants' quarters

West African trade

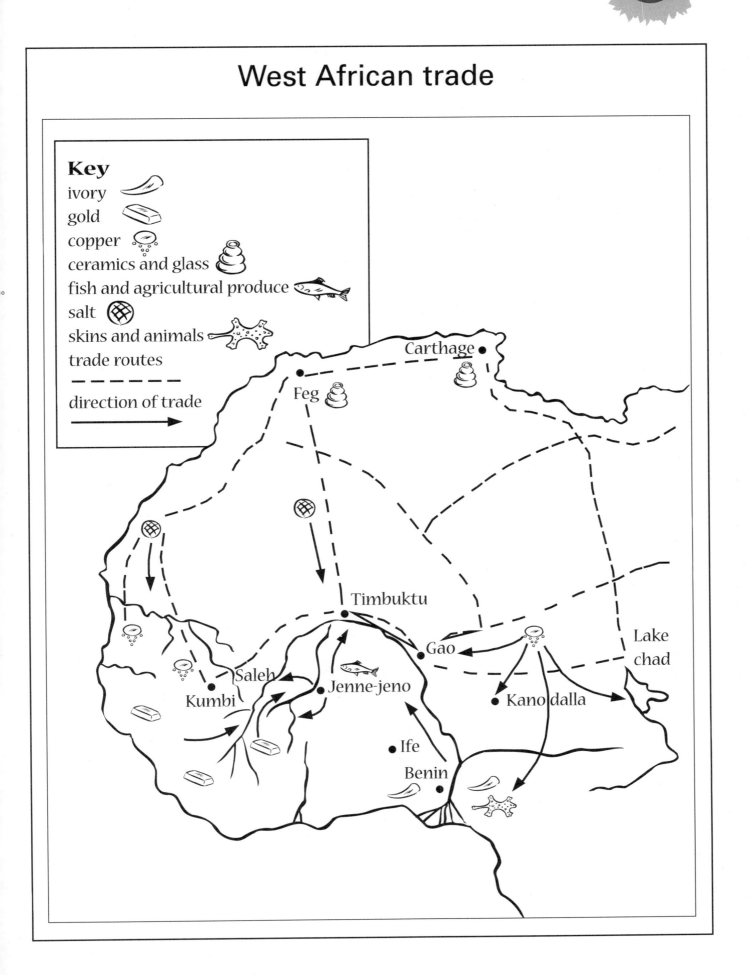

Key
ivory
gold
copper
ceramics and glass
fish and agricultural produce
salt
skins and animals
trade routes
- - - - - - -
direction of trade
⟶

Carthage

Feg

Timbuktu

Gao

Lake chad

Saleh
Kumbi
Jenne-jeno
Kano dalla

Ife
Benin

PHOTOCOPIABLE

The Benin Empire – geographical features

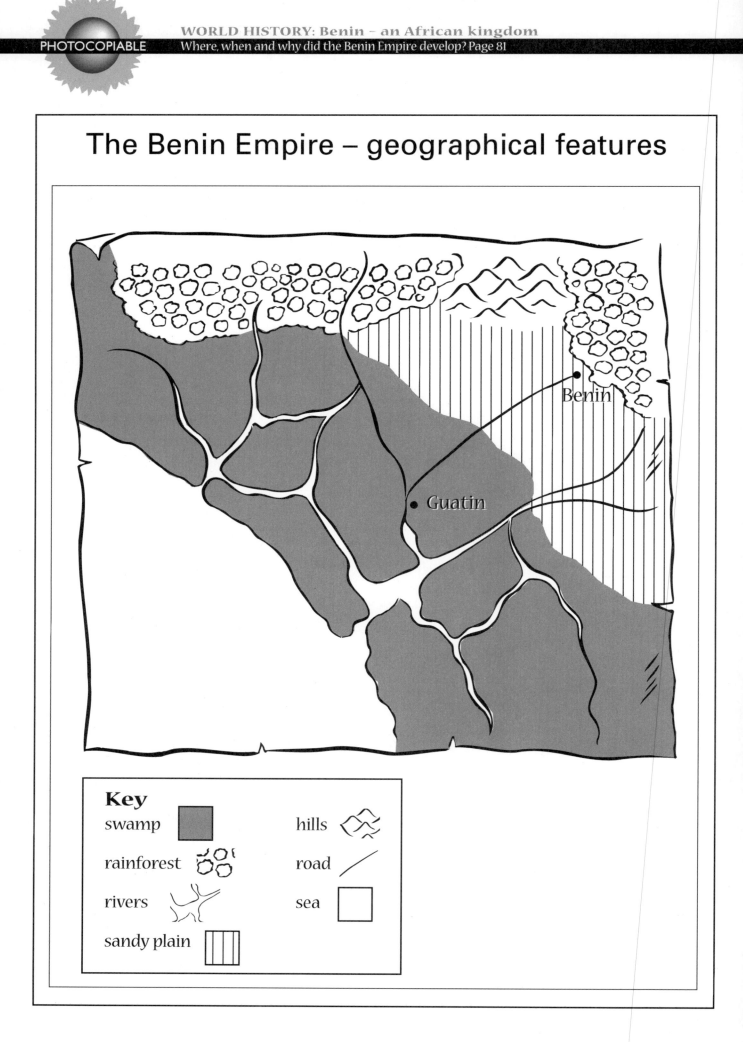

Key

swamp

rainforest

rivers

sandy plain

hills

road

sea

Benin

Guatin

PHOTOCOPIABLE

Name _____   Date _____

Benin – an African kingdom

Think about what you have found out about how Benin came to be an important and powerful state in the 16th century.
Give three reasons for the Benin Empire becoming so successful.
Explain why you think this.

●

●

●

On the timeline below mark when you think the kingdom of Benin was flourishing.

Celtic   Romans   Anglo-Saxons   Vikings   Middle Ages   Tudors   Georgians   Victorians   Present day

On the map below show roughly where you think Benin City was found.

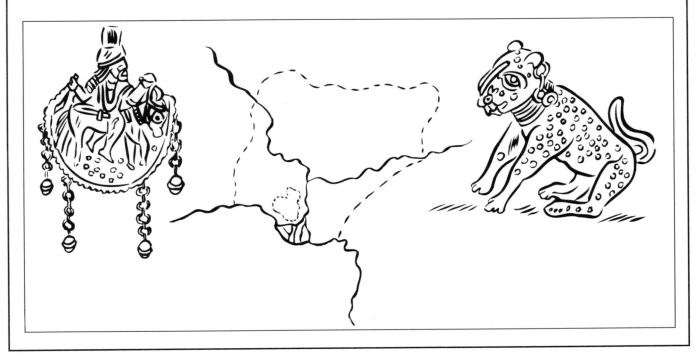

WORLD HISTORY: Benin- an African kingdom

PHOTOCOPIABLE   What was the city like? Page 83

Contemporary accounts of Benin City

"The houses are large and the people live in such security that they have no doors to their houses. The house of the Oba is richly decorated with fine columns and the city is industrious, well governed and wealthy."

Written in 1694 by a Portuguese captain – Lourenco Pinto

"The streets are very broad and long. Markets are kept in them continually. Houses are covered on the top with reeds, straw or leaves placed. The houses are large and handsome with their polished clay walls. The long wide streets are kept very neat as every woman cleans her own doorstep."

Written in 1702 by a dutch trader – Van Nyendael

"The town seems to be very great. When you enter into it you go into a great broad street. This is not paved but is several times broader than some of the streets in Amsterdam. The street goes straight through the town and never crooks. When you are in the great main street you see many other great streets going off to the sides. The houses in this time stand in good order, close and even with each other, much as the houses in Holland stand. Houses of the wealthy have two or three steps up from the street. In the front is a courtyard where one might sit in the dry. The gallery is cleaned each morning by slaves who also spread straw mats for sitting on. Houses are broad with long galleries inside and divided into many rooms. These rooms are four-square. Over them they have a roof that is open in the middle so that the rain and wind and light come in. Here they sleep and eat their meals although they have other little houses besides for kitchens and other rooms. The walls are made of red clay. These are made as smooth as mirrors with washing and rubbing, although it sometimes happens that a heavy rain comes and it washes down the walls. It gives them much to do.

Common houses are not built the same. They have but one straight wall in the middle of which there is a wooden door. Air and daylight come in through the roof for they do not make windows."

Written in 1600 by a Dutch trader – name unknown

The Oba of Benin

Name _____ Date _____

The Oba of Benin

Briefly describe what you see in your picture:

Words to describe the Oba	Why do you think this?	What do you think now?

Complete the following statement:

We think that the Oba was/was not an important person because…

The Oba of Benin

Symbols associated with the Oba

Red Coral – a symbol of royalty and royal favour. Only the royal family and their favorites could wear coral. The more you had the more important you were.

Ivory – a sign of wealth. The Oba also controlled who could buy and sell this commodity.

Leopards – a sign of royalty. The leopards ruled over the jungle as the Oba ruled over his empire.

Mudfish – a sign of power. The mudfish lived on land and in water and this was used to show how the Oba ruled over both water and land.

Sword – a symbol of authority. The Oba's word was law and he could decide who lived or died.

Large eyes – a sign of beauty.

Large cotton skirt – this was sometimes used to hide the fact that the Oba was supposed to have feet of fish to show his divinity and his control over both land and water. The Oba was directly related to the gods and was therefore not like ordinary men.

The Oba's size – the Oba was often depicted as being larger than his attendants to demonstrate his importance.

WORLD HISTORY: Benin – an African kingdom
What was the market like? Page 87

PHOTOCOPIABLE

Osasere and the 'Strangers'

Osasere hurried past the tall, red-walled houses on her way to the market place. Normally she tried to move with poise and presence, as benefitted one whose father was a well-known artist. Today, however, was not a day for calm. Osasere's father was a brass caster, one of the famous craftsmen of Benin City. Usually he worked exclusively for the Oba and his court, but he had recently been given permission to make something for the strange, pale visitors from the distant northern lands. Today they were coming to her father's stall in the market to talk about what they wanted. Osasere wanted to see what they really looked like for she had heard that they were not the same as 'real people'.

The sun was not yet high in the sky but already the market was full of bustle. Osasere skidded past a crowd of women potters gossiping and laughing as they carried in their terracotta pots on long poles from their villages outside the city walls. Little black cooking stoves were heating up as women crouched over them, nursing embers into life. Osasere could smell the appetising aromas of goat stew and fried plantain. She ran past the leatherworkers' stalls and those of the woodcarvers and those of the ivory carvers. Today was not a day for stopping to look at the tiny ivory comb she had always wanted. She flashed past stalls loaded with bolts of blue, handwoven cloth brought down from the north. She slowed to wave to the old Nosarievme who sat in the shade of a large tree watching the children of the stallholders. They were crouched at her feet, listening open-mouthed to her stories. Normally Osasere would have joined them, but not today.

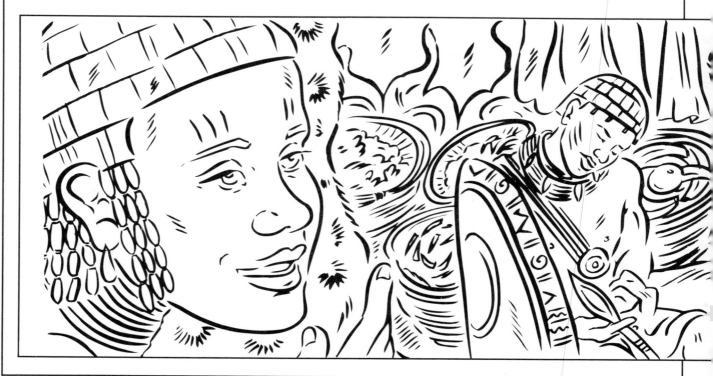

Osasere loved the market. It was so full of noise and colour. Mounds of brightly coloured fruit and vegetables, red hot peppers, brown and knobbly yams, giant hands of yellow bananas and hard green ochra lay piled everywhere on raffia mats or the packed red ground. The live chickens, goats, monkeys and dogs added to the noise and excitement. Osasere stopped to finger a beautiful leopard skin, so golden, so soft, and smiled shyly up at the tall muscled huntsman who sat silently polishing his spear.

Ahead Osasere could see the poles of her father's stall. Suddenly she noticed the foreign traders. They were a very strange sight indeed. Osasere wondered what shape their legs were as she looked at the peculiar puffed-up cloth they wrapped around their legs. They also wore thick, heavy cloth jackets as well as fine white shirts. Soon as the heat of the day grew, they would become very hot.

"Maybe that is why some of them are a curious red colour," thought Osasere as she looked at one of the warriors who seemed to be wearing a metal turtle shell on his chest. "Perhaps he is already cooking to death!"

Osasere did not like the strangers' pasty white skin, thin noses and small pale eyes. "Could they be the same colour all over?" she wondered. One looked more like an animal than a man with thick black fur all over his face. Osasere hid on the edge of the crowd and watched the northerners talk to her father. She looked at her own smooth, supple, rich brown skin and pitied the foreigners. They were very far from home and so different from everyone around them. "Even though they are rich and are friends with the all-powerful Oba, they must feel very alone," thought Osasere sadly. Her father would need to be a great artist indeed to make a true picture of these strange newcomers.

WORLD HISTORY: Benin – an African kingdom
What was the market like? Page 87
PHOTOCOPIABLE

Name _____ Date _____

The market in Benin (1)

You are one of the European visitors.
Look at the Tudor reference books to see what sort of clothes you might wear and how you might look. Think about the sort of person you are.

● Are you one of the noblemen sent as an ambassador to the Oba? What sort of goods will you be wanting to take back to your king or queen?

● Are you one of the merchants keen to bring back exotic goods? What have you got to trade and what are you hoping to buy?

● Are you one of the soldiers or sailors accompanying the merchants? Will you look for spears or swords while talking to some of the Oba's warriors? Perhaps you are looking for a small trinket to take back to your wife or mother. What sort of thing do you think she would like?

You may have one or two noblemen, four or five merchants in your group, and the rest of the group must be soldiers or sailors.

Write some notes to describe your character.

Name _____   Date _____

The market in Benin (2)

You are one of the stall-holders at the market.

Look at the reference books to see what sort of clothes you might wear and how you might look. Look at pictures of the type of market goods that were sold in old Benin. You could also look at photos or pictures of markets in modern Nigeria. Think about the sort of person you are.

● Are you a man or a woman?
● Are you young or old?
● What do you look like?
● What sort of clothes do you wear?
● What type of goods do you sell?

Chose one of the following stalls:

Female stall-holders	Male stall-holders
Potters – terracotta or iron Clothworkers Vegetable, fruit or foodstuff sellers Pepper sellers Cooks Raffia mat makers	Ivory carvers Leatherworkers Bronze casters Ironworkers Woodcarvers Huntsmen

Write some notes to describe your character.

WORLD HISTORY: Benin – an African kingdom
What was the market like? Page 87
PHOTOCOPIABLE

Name _____   Date _____

The market in Benin (3)

You have come to the market to buy something.
Look at the reference books to see what sort of clothes you might wear and how you might look. Look at pictures of the type of market goods that were sold in old Benin. You could also look at photos or pictures of markets in modern Nigeria. Think about the sort of person you are.

- Are you a man or a woman?
- Are you young or old?
- What do you look like?
- What sort of clothes do you wear?
- What sort of thing do you want to buy?
- How much money have you got?
- Have you come to buy food?
- Are you one of the Oba's chiefs or officials? (You may only have one or two in the group.) What sort of thing do you think the Oba might want or need?
- Have you come to buy a weapon?
- Do you need something for your home?

Write some notes on the back of this sheet to describe your character.

WORLD HISTORY: Benin – an African kingdom
Why was storytelling important? Page 88
PHOTOCOPIABLE

Eware and the Portraits of Bronze

Storyteller *"Tohio"* I greet you all – give me your attention.
People *"Hiahia kpo"* Go ahead, we have given you our attention.
Storyteller *"Okha okpa nadore…"* There came a day…, or Then came a story…

There came a day when the Oba Eware was drawing near to the end of his long, illustrious life. Although he was no longer as vigorous as he had been, people still came to him to bring gifts in remembrance of his great acts of the past. They came to ask his advice for he had ruled long and wisely for thirty years and was still rich and powerful.

The Oba wanted to leave his people with a lasting memory of himself and his reign. He thought long and hard before deciding to leave them a portrait of himself to remind them of Eware the Great and to encourage them to carry on his powerful rule.

What material should he use? Wood? The ants would eat it and the damp would rot it and soon the portrait would be gone.

The portrait must be made of metal, thought the Oba at last, for nothing destroys metal, but he could not decide which metal to use.

Should it be iron or bronze?

At this time, the ironworkers were a great and important guild. They were keen to receive the honour and so immortalise their great king. The bronze casters also wanted to celebrate their king's reign. The Oba thought hard again and decided that both should have the honour. He would hold a competition and whichever guild was able to produce the best portrait would be the winner. The iron workers were great craftsmen. They made bells and the ceremonial swords that the warriors carried. They made the knives and tools of everyday life, the cooking pots and the hoes that turned the land. The bronze casters' guild knew that they would need to think of something very special and met together to make a cunning plan.

For months the two guilds worked on the portraits. Their fires roared, their bellows puffed and their hammers rang. At last they were finished and each guild carried their offering to the Oba to show him the fruits of their labours. The people greeted the craftsmen with great celebrations. There was music and dancing. The beat of the drums matched the pounding of the dancers' feet. The metal workers danced too. The iron workers danced the rhythm of their hammers on the anvils. The bronze casters danced the rhythm of their bellows pumping the fire.

At the main courtyard in the Oba's palace, the chief of the iron workers knelt in front of Eware. He touched his forehead to the ground three times. He held the portrait high. The people gasped when they saw the beauty and the craftsmanship. It showed the Oba at the height of his power with all his strength and wisdom. A great cheer rose up.

Then the leader of the bronze casters came forward and bowed low. He called for three of his workers. There were three portraits. The first showed Eware as a young man, handsome and proud. The second showed Eware in his middle years, strong and powerful. The last portrait showed the Oba as an old man, wise and dignified.

The Oba was delighted and turned to congratulate the leader of the bronze casters.

"You have shown me as I was and as I am now," he said. "People will remember me for the great deeds of my youth. They will think of me when I was at the height of my powers. They will not laugh at my frailty in old age as they will see wisdom and experience. The competition goes to the bronze casters guild."

The people cheered and danced their praise. The celebrations went on long into the night. The only people not celebrating were the iron workers, who felt disgraced. The power of the bronze casters' guild grew and grew until it was one of the most important of all the guilds.

Storyteller *"Evba okha na ya dewu"* That is where the story dies.
"Okhanireren ghi gbemwen, okhanimaren ghigbemwen" The story I know won't kill me, the story I don't know won't kill me.

(Adapted from *Benin, An African Kingdom*, The Storybook, retold by Deborah Isaacs and Elizabeth Isaacs, the Educational Television Company; the traditional format for the storytelling comes from *Benin, An African Kingdom*, Cathy Midwinter WWF UK)

WORLD HISTORY: Benin – an African kingdom

How do we know about Benin's past? Page 90

PHOTOCOPIABLE

Name _____   Date _____

How to find out about the past

Examine your evidence carefully.

Source 1
What type of evidence do you have?

What sort of information does it give you?

What is it good for?

What doesn't it tell you, or what isn't it good for?

Source 2
What type of evidence do you have?

What sort of information does it give you?

What is it good for?

What doesn't it tell you, or what isn't it good for?

159

PHOTOCOPIABLE

Name _____ Date _____

Source 3

What type of evidence do you have?

What sort of information does it give you?

What is it good for?

What doesn't it tell you, or what isn't it good for?

Now that you have examined all the evidence:

Did you think any one piece of evidence was better than the others? If so why?

Were there any pieces of evidence that were not useful? Why do you think this?

Why do you think the work of archaeologists is important?

What have you found out about using evidence?